D0426356

A Classic Christmas

A Classic Christmas

Spiritual Reflections, Timeless Literature,
and Treasured Verse & Scripture

HarperOne

Content developed by Mark Gilroy Creative, LLC. www.markgilroy.com
Packaged with Thinkpen Design, Inc. www.thinkpendesign.com

All interior images Copyright © 2009 Jupiter Images

HarperCollins books may be purchased for educational, business, or sales promotional use. For information please write: Special Markets Department, HarperCollins Publishers, 10 East 53rd Street, New York, NY 10022.

HarperCollins Web site: http://www.harpercollins.com
Harper Collins®, 📖®, and HarperOne™ are
trademarks of HarperCollins Publishers.

FIRST EDITION

Library of Congress Cataloging-in-Publication Data is available upon request.
ISBN 978-0-06-189387-2

09 10 11 12 13 SCPC 10 9 8 7 6 5 4 3 2 1

Table of Contents

Peace

Journey

Giving

Joy

The Gift

What Is a Classic Christmas?

Every year, December arrives and urges us to enjoy the merriment of Christmas—the music, the presents, the once-a-year culinary treats. And every year, it calls us back to years gone by. We can't think of Christmas without thinking about the holidays we loved as children, or about the ancient roots of some of our most beloved traditions, or about that very old story about the baby and the angels and the wise men. So what makes a modern Christmas classic? What gives it that rich, time-tested quality?

Some version of a winter holiday has been around for centuries—millennia, even. Most ancient cultures celebrated the winter solstice. (Notably, evergreens tended to be featured heavily in these celebrations.) The Roman version of this festival was called Saturnalia, during which people took a break from work, ate and drank a lot, gave presents, and gambled freely.

Saturnalia was around for almost two hundred years before the birth of Christ and before the establishment of the Christian church around 60 A.D., and thus before Christmas, the celebration of Christ's Nativity. And for the first few centuries, Christians didn't even celebrate the Nativity. It was added to the church calendar only in 354 A.D., and the date selected probably had little to do with when the Christ child was actually born. The chosen date of

December 25 fell at the end of Saturnalia, a time when people were already celebrating that winter solstice anyway. (Plus, that date was reserved to celebrate the sun god, Sol Invictus, who was associated with the emperor; linking the religious holiday with the political one may have been a play to curry the emperor's favor.)

Since then, Christmas has enjoyed a vibrant and varying history, both as a religious and semi-religious observance. Medieval Christmas was a wild celebration with revelry of all levels of depravity. The pendulum swung the other way with the Protestant Reformation, when Christmas was all but abolished in many churches. The Puritans, too, frowned on Christmas in the early American colonies, while some denominations kept up the observance of the Nativity.

So how did December 25 become the holiday we know and love today? Many of our Christmas traditions evolved somewhat piecemeal. Saint Nicholas became the familiar version of Santa Claus with the help of 1800s literature. Writer Washington Irving adapted the old story of Sinterklaas and created the idea of the flying sleigh and presents delivered via chimney. Clement C. Moore took it one step further with his 1823 poem, "A Visit from Saint Nicholas." The Christmas tree is said to have arrived in English-speaking Christmas traditions through Prince Albert of Germany (though those evergreen decorations were hardly new). Likewise, the poinsettia became a Christmas standard after Joel Roberts

Poinsett, an ambassador to Mexico, brought the plant into the United States in 1828 (it blooms in winter, making it a good floral decoration for Christmas).

As time went on, traditions took hold and spread, partly due to advancements in transportation, and Christmas became more and more popular, with more denominations welcoming it back onto their calendars. In 1870, Ulysses S. Grant officially recognized Christmas as a civil holiday.

So after several centuries of a deeply-ingrained annual tradition of revelry; the force of marketing associated with gifts, cards, and holiday treats; and a little political maneuvering, Christmas became the cultural phenomenon we know it to be. But along the way, it also encompassed the best things about being human, things like giving and goodness and the warmth of food, friends, and family. And it continually reminded us of the evocative story of the baby in the manger.

What makes for a classic Christmas? Well, it's not exactly the history of the holiday, though that's certainly part of it. And it's not just the turn of the phrase, a clever thought, a cheerful whimsy, a centuries-old hymn, or some other form of timeless writing. What makes Christmas classic is the message found in the birth of a Baby and your open heart. ✧

Christmas was foretold centuries before the
birth of Christ. Is it any wonder that the
Christmas season is filled with anticipation?

For a child has been born for us,
a son given to us.

—Isaiah 9:6

From the City of Bethlehem

But you, O Bethlehem of Ephrathah,
who are one of the little clans of Judah,
from you shall come forth for me one who is to rule in Israel,
whose origin is from of old,
from ancient days.

And he shall stand and feed his flock in the strength of the
LORD, in the majesty of the name of the LORD his God.
And they shall live secure, for now he shall be great
to the ends of the earth;
and he shall be the one of peace.

—Micah 5:2, 4–5

Swaddling Clothes

Karl Barth

And this will be a sign for you; you will find a babe wrapped in swaddling clothes and lying in a manger.

—LUKE 2:12 RSV

That the shepherds of Bethlehem will find the child "wrapped in swaddling clothes and lying in a manger" is, according to the sacred text, to be a sign for them that this child is the Savior, Christ the Lord, and that peace has been established between God in the highest and man on earth. Thus man has received definite and real counsel, direction and hope. Of all this the swaddling clothes and the manger are to be the "sign." How strange, for the swaddling clothes and the manger speak of segregation, poverty, oppression and need. "This will be a sign for you." Who would look here for the wonder that God in the highest and man on earth have really and truly become one? Does this sign not speak of the very opposite, of divine wrath, human impotence, and the deep dilemma in which man spends his days without consolation, direction and help? But it means exactly what it says: "This will be a sign for you," here is the wonder, here is the Savior of all who seek help.

The old Church was right when she found the concealment of divine revelation declared in this text. Luther in particular was right when he interpreted the swaddling clothes and the manger as the Holy Scripture of the Old Testament, in which Christ was revealed, but revealed in concealment. It speaks from beginning to end of a covenant between God and man. But this God in all His deeds is the holy, hard and angry God, and man in all his deeds is the selfwilled man, impotent in his selfwill. The Old Testament does not reach the point where peace is concluded between God and man. This event, which promises the covenant between God and His people, is not realized in the Old Testament. In a sense it is revealed in the Old Testament too, but it is concealed under something which might be understood as its opposite. The Old Testament is only the sign of its own truth. Christ is only "prophesied": "You will find a child wrapped in swaddling clothes and lying in a manger."

Whoever seeks divine revelation, will seek in vain, unless he follows this sign. One can and must be content with this: revelation is never present where we expect to see heaven on earth, or a glorified earth and God in harmony and even in union with man. Revelation never has a recognizable form, its wisdom and power can never be proved, its triumph is never apparent, its success is not tangible and its benefit not for immediate enjoyment. Certainly these things do exist; but if one insists on seeing revelation in them, one must clearly understand that what one sees there, is certainly not divine revelation. To be divine it must first be concealed. Divine revelation is the opening of a door which can be unlocked only from the inside, not from the outside. We can only discover the sign, but not Him who is "true God and true man." We can discover only the "swaddling clothes" and the "manger" of Bethlehem and the "Cross" of Golgotha. We cannot discover the consolation, the direction and the hope which Christ grants to us; we can discover our own lack of all these things and our own contradiction against them, but we cannot discover the God who asks us why we lack all these things and why we contradict Him so violently. We can not discover even this sign unless it is given to us as truly as the Old Testament is given. With Law and Prophets at our side we can learn to see that it is set in the midst of our life.

Whoever holds on to the sign, finds divine revelation; he comes to Christ the Lord and receives consolation, direction, and hope. Can one really say this so definitely and positively? Yes, it is there definitely and positively, written in Holy Scripture: "You will find a child." It was not just anybody, but the Angel of the Lord who said this, and one can say it after him. Surely one can listen to the Angel of the Lord and take it from him: You will find him—not only the sign, but that which the sign signifies, "a child wrapped in swaddling clothes and lying in a manger." Anyone who really holds on to the sign, undistracted and unerringly, may be assured quite definitely and positively that he is on the way to God's revelation, he will find it. The concealment which is described by this sign is not some mystery, some riddle or some paradox, but the concealment of God, the concealment of His revelation. He who without blinking and without being distracted by so-called "revelations" looked only in the direction of the sign, would already find the divine revelation. He would stand on the circumference which must unfailingly lead to this point. Why must we say this in subjunctives and conditional sentences? They really mean the indicative, the unconditional sentence: You will find! The sign is all right, and Christ the Lord whom the sign signifies, is all right. But do we really take in what the Angel of the Lord says to us, and take it from him as from the Angel of the Lord? This indeed is the condition for applying to us the whole indicative mood of the Christmas message "You will find." If this condition is not fulfilled, then we are not on that circumference and cannot possibly reach that goal. This is the only condition which we can and must have. However, we cannot create it. Who can create the condition in which he can truly, earnestly, and without wavering hold on to the covenant between God and man, in which the desired peace is always concealed? Does not everything speak against it? Is it not essential that the wonder of revelation should have already taken place in a person so that man can really hold on to this sign?

Why should not this condition be fulfilled already? Why should not the indicative of Christmas indicate even this—that we do not stand outside, beholding the great wonder like the portal of a Gothic cathedral, but are already inside? Why should we not really repeat what the Angel of the Lord has said and take it as from the Angel of the Lord: "You will find"?

If we do this, then we have already reached the mysterious midway between the sign and Him whom the sign signifies. I can say this as the ultimate truth, and all who read this can take it as ultimate truth: "to you is born this day a Savior." Can I really say this? Yes, with God in the highest nothing is impossible, neither with men on earth with whom He is well pleased.✧

KARL BARTH (1886–1968) WAS A GERMAN THEOLOGIAN WHO IS CONSID-ERED THE FATHER OF NEO-ORTHODOXY IN PROTESTANT THEOLOGY. THIS SELECTION IS TAKEN FROM A SERIES OF CHRISTMAS MEDITATIONS THAT APPEARED IN GERMAN DAILY NEWSPAPERS BETWEEN 1926 AND 1933.

The Angel Appears to Mary

In the sixth month the angel Gabriel was sent by God to a town in Galilee called Nazareth, to a virgin engaged to a man whose name was Joseph, of the house of David. The virgin's name was Mary. And he came to her and said, "Greetings, favored one! The Lord is with you." But she was much perplexed by his words and pondered what sort of greeting this might be. The angel said to her, "Do not be afraid, Mary, for you have found favor with God. And now, you will conceive in your womb and bear a son, and you will name him Jesus. He will be great, and will be called the Son of the Most High, and the Lord God will give to him the throne of his ancestor David. He will reign over the house of Jacob forever, and of his kingdom there will be no end." Mary said to the angel, "How can this be, since I am a virgin?" The angel said to her, "The Holy Spirit will come upon you, and the power of the Most High will overshadow you; therefore the child to be born will be holy; he will be called Son of God. And now, your relative Elizabeth in her old age has also conceived a son; and this is the sixth month for her who was said to be barren. For nothing will be impossible with God." Then Mary said, "Here am I, the servant of the Lord; let it be with me according to your word." Then the angel departed from her.

—LUKE 1:26–38

The authentically hopeful Christmas
spirit has not looked away from the darkness, but
straight into it. The true and victorious Christmas
spirit does not look away from death, but directly
at it. Advent begins in the dark.

Fleming Rutledge

The Servant of the Lord

The spirit of the LORD GOD is upon me,
because the LORD has anointed me;
he has sent me to bring good news to the oppressed,
to bind up the brokenhearted,
to proclaim liberty to the captives,
and release to the prisoners;
to proclaim the year of the LORD's favor,
and the day of vengeance of our God;
to comfort all who mourn;
to provide for those who mourn in Zion—
to give them a garland instead of ashes,
the oil of gladness instead of mourning,
the mantle of praise instead of a faint spirit.
They will be called oaks of righteousness,
the planting of the LORD, to display his glory.

—ISAIAH 61:1–3

The Messenger

Many associate these passages in Isaiah and Malachi with John the Baptist, Jesus' relative. John ministered in the desert and called people to repentance; he even baptized Jesus in the Jordan. He was said to prepare the way for Jesus' own ministry.

A voice cries out:
"In the wilderness prepare the way of the LORD,
make straight in the desert a highway for our God.
Every valley shall be lifted up,
and every mountain and hill be made low;
the uneven ground shall become level,
and the rough places a plain.
Then the glory of the LORD shall be revealed,
and all people shall see it together,
for the mouth of the LORD has spoken."

—ISAIAH 40:3–5

See, I am sending my messenger to prepare the way before me,
and the LORD whom you seek will suddenly come to his temple.
The messenger of the covenant in whom you delight—indeed, he is
coming, says the LORD of the hosts.

—MALACHI 3:1

In the beginning was the Word, and the Word was with God, and the Word was God. He was in the beginning with God. All things came into being through him, and without him not one thing came into being. What has come into being in him was life, and the life was the light of all people. The light shines in the darkness, and the darkness did not overcome it.

There was a man sent from God, whose name was John. He came as a witness to testify to the light, so that all might believe through him. He himself was not the light, but he came to testify to the light. The true light, which enlightens everyone, was coming into the world.

He was in the world, and the world came into being through him; yet the world did not know him. He came to what was his own, and his own people did not accept him. But to all who received him, who believed in his name, he gave power to become children of God, who were born, not of blood or of the will of the flesh or of the will of man, but of God.

And the Word became flesh and lived among us, and we have seen his glory, the glory as of a father's only son, full of grace and truth.

—JOHN 1:1–14

The First Christmas Tree

Eugene Field

1901

O nce upon a time the forest was in a great commotion. Early in the evening the wise old cedars had shaken their heads ominously and predicted strange things. They had lived in the forest many, many years; but never had they seen such marvelous sights as were to be seen now in the sky, and upon the hills, and in the distant village.

"Pray tell us what you see," pleaded a little vine; "we who are not as tall as you can behold none of these wonderful things. Describe them to us, that we may enjoy them with you."

"I am filled with such amazement," said one of the cedars, "that I can hardly speak. The whole sky seems to be aflame, and the stars appear to be dancing among the clouds; angels walk down from heaven to earth, and enter the village or talk with the shepherds upon the hills."

The vine listened in mute astonishment. Such things never before had happened. The vine trembled with excitement. Its nearest neighbor was a tiny tree, so small it scarcely ever was noticed; yet it was a very beautiful little tree, and the vines and ferns and mosses and other humble residents of the forest loved it dearly.

"How I should like to see the angels!" sighed the little tree, "and how I should like to see the stars dancing among the clouds! It must be very beautiful."

As the vine and the little tree talked of these things, the cedars watched with increasing interest the wonderful scenes over and beyond the confines of the forest. Presently they thought they heard music, and they were not mistaken, for soon the whole air was full of the sweetest harmonies ever heard upon earth.

"What beautiful music!" cried the little tree. "I wonder whence it comes."

"The angels are singing," said a cedar; "for none but angels could make such sweet music."

"But the stars are singing, too," said another cedar; "yes, and the shepherds on the hill join in the song, and what a strangely glorious song it is!"

The trees listened to the singing, but they did not understand its meaning: it seemed to be an anthem, and it was of a Child who had been born; but further than this they did not understand. The strange and glorious song continued all the night; and all that night the angels walked to and fro, and the shepherd-folk talked with the angels, and the stars danced and caroled in high heaven. And it was nearly morning when the cedars cried out, "They are coming to the forest! the angels are coming to the forest!" And, surely enough, this was true. The vine and the little tree were very terrified, and they begged their older and stronger neighbors to protect them from harm. But the cedars were too busy with their own fears to pay any heed to the faint pleadings of the humble vine and the little tree.

The angels came into the forest, singing the same glorious anthem about the Child, and the stars sang in chorus with them, until every part of the woods rang with echoes of that wondrous song. There was nothing in the appearance of this angel host to inspire fear; they were clad all in white, and there were crowns upon their fair heads, and golden harps in their hands; love, hope, charity, compassion, and joy beamed from their beautiful faces, and their presence seemed to fill the forest with a divine peace. The angels came through the forest to where the little tree stood, and gathering around it, they touched it with their hands, and kissed its little branches, and sang even more sweetly than before. And their song was about the Child, the Child, the Child who had been born. Then the stars came down from the skies and danced and hung upon the branches of the tree, and they, too, sang that song—the song of the Child. And all the other trees and the vines and the ferns and the mosses beheld in wonder; nor could they understand why all these things were being done, and why this exceeding honor should be shown to the little tree.

When the morning came the angels left the forest—all but one angel, who remained behind and lingered near the little tree. Then a cedar asked: "Why do you tarry with us, holy angel?" And the angel answered: "I stay to guard this little tree, for it is sacred, and no harm shall come to it."

The little tree felt quite relieved by this assurance, and it held up its head more confidently than ever before. And how it thrived and grew, and waxed in strength and beauty! The cedars said they never had seen the like. The sun seemed to lavish its choicest rays upon the little tree, heaven dropped its sweetest dew upon it, and the winds never came to the forest that they did not forget their rude manners and linger to kiss the little tree and sing it their prettiest songs. No danger ever menaced it, no harm threatened; for the angel never slept—through the day and through the night the angel watched the little tree and protected it from all evil. Oftentimes the trees talked with the angel; but of course they understood little of what he said, for he spoke always of the Child who was to become the Master; and always when thus he talked, he caressed the little tree, and stroked its branches and leaves, and moistened them with his tears. It was all so very strange that none in the forest could understand.

So the years passed, the angel watching his blooming charge. Sometimes the beasts strayed down toward the little tree and threatened to devour its tender foliage; sometimes the woodman came with his axe, intent upon hewing down the straight and comely thing; sometimes the hot, consuming breath of drought swept from the south, and sought to blight the forest and all its verdure: the angel kept them from the little tree. Serene and beautiful it grew, until now it was no longer a little tree, but the pride and glory of the forest.

One day the tree heard someone coming through the forest. Hitherto the angel had hastened to its side when men approached; but now the angel strode away and stood under the cedars yonder.

"Dear angel," cried the tree, "can you not hear the footsteps of someone approaching? Why do you leave me?"

"Have no fear," said the angel; "for he who comes is the Master."

The Master came to the tree and beheld it. He placed his hands upon its smooth trunk and branches; and the tree was thrilled with a strange and glorious delight. Then he stooped and kissed the tree, and then he turned and went away.

Many times after that the Master came to the forest, and when he came it always was to where the tree stood. Many times he rested beneath the tree and enjoyed the shade of its foliage, and listened to the music of the wind as it swept through the rustling leaves. Many times he slept there, and the tree watched over him, and the forest was still, and all its voices were hushed. And the angel hovered near like a faithful sentinel.

Ever and anon men came with the Master to the forest, and sat with him in the shade of the tree, and talked with him of matters which the tree never could understand; only it heard that the talk was of love and charity and gentleness, and it saw that the Master was beloved and venerated by the others. It heard them tell of the Master's goodness and humility—how he had healed the sick and raised the dead and bestowed inestimable blessings wherever he walked. And the tree loved the Master for his beauty and his goodness; and when he came to the forest it was full of joy, but when he came not it was sad. And the other trees of the forest joined in its happiness and its sorrow, for they, too, loved the Master. And the angel always hovered near.

The Master came one night alone into the forest, and his face was pale with anguish and wet with tears, and he fell upon his knees and prayed. The tree heard him, and all the forest was still, as if it were standing in the presence of death. And when the morning came, lo! The angel had gone.

Then there was a great confusion in the forest. There was a sound of rude voices, and a clashing of swords and staves. Strange men appeared, uttering loud oaths and cruel threats, and the tree was filled with terror. It called for the angel, but the angel came not.

"Alas," cried the vine, "they have come to destroy the tree, the pride and glory of the forest!"

The forest was sorely agitated, but it was in vain. The strange men plied their axes with cruel vigor, and the tree was hewn to the ground. Its beautiful branches were cut away and cast aside, and its soft, thick foliage was strewn to the tenderer mercies of the winds.

"They are killing me!" cried the tree; "why is not the angel here to protect me?"

But no one heard the piteous cry—none but the other trees of the forest, and they wept, and the little vine wept too.

Then the cruel men dragged the despoiled and hewn tree from the forest; and the forest saw that beauteous thing no more.

But the night wind that swept down from the City of the Great King that night to ruffle the bosom of distant Galilee, tarried in the forest awhile to say that it had seen that day a cross upraised on Calvary—the tree on which was stretched the body of the dying Master. ✧

EUGENE FIELD (1850–1895) WAS AN AMERICAN JOURNALIST AND WRITER BEST KNOWN FOR CHILDREN'S POEMS AND STORIES, PERHAPS THE MOST FAMOUS OF WHICH IS "WYNKEN, BLYNKEN, AND NOD." "THE FIRST CHRISTMAS TREE" WAS PUBLISHED POSTHUMOUSLY IN *A Little Book of Profitable Tales*.

The Good Shepherd

Get you up to a high mountain,
O Zion, herald of good tidings;
lift up your voice with strength,
O Jerusalem, herald of good tidings,
lift it up, do not fear;
say to the cities of Judah,
"Here is your God!"
See, the LORD GOD comes with might,
and his arm rules for him;
his reward is with him,
and his recompense before him.
He will feed his flock like a shepherd;
he will gather the lambs in his arms,
and carry them in his bosom,
and gently lead the mother sheep.

—ISAIAH 40:9–11

The Prince of Peace

Shout aloud and sing for joy, O royal Zion,
for great in your midst is the Holy One of Israel.

—ISAIAH 12:6

A shoot shall come out from the stump of Jesse,
and a branch shall grow out of his roots.
The spirit of the LORD shall rest on him,
the spirit of wisdom and understanding,
the spirit of counsel and might,
the spirit of knowledge and the fear of the LORD.
His delight shall be in the fear of the LORD.

He shall not judge by what his eyes see,
or decide by what his ears hear;
but with righteousness he shall judge the poor,
and decide with equity for the meek of the earth;
he shall strike the earth with the rod of his mouth,
and with the breath of his lips he shall kill the wicked. . .

The wolf shall live with the lamb,
the leopard shall lie down the kid,
the calf and the lion and the fatling together,
and a little child shall lead them.

—ISAIAH 12:1–4, 6

They will not hurt or destroy
on all my holy mountain;
for the earth will be full of the knowledge of the LORD
as the waters cover the sea.

—ISAIAH 12:9

Christmas Everywhere

Phillips Brooks

1903

Everywhere, everywhere, Christmas tonight!
Christmas in lands of the fir-tree and pine,
Christmas in lands of the palm-tree and vine,
Christmas where snow peaks stand solemn and white,
Christmas where cornfields stand sunny and bright.
Everywhere, everywhere, Christmas tonight!

Christmas where children are hopeful and gay,
Christmas where old men are patient and gray,
Christmas where peace, like a dove in his flight,
Broods o're brave men in the thick of the fight;
Everywhere, everywhere, Christmas tonight!

For the Christ-child who comes is the Master of all;
No palace too great, no cottage too small.
The Angels who welcome Him sing from the height,
"In the city of David, a King in His might."
Everywhere, everywhere, Christmas tonight.

Then let every heart keep its Christmas within,
Christ's pity for sorrow, Christ's hatred for sin,
Christ's care for the weakest, Christ's courage for right,
Christ's dread for darkness, Christ's love of the light,
Everywhere, everywhere, Christmas tonight!

So the stars of the midnight which compass us round
Shall see a strange glory, and hear a sweet sound,
And cry, "Look! the earth is aflame with delight,
O sons of the morning, rejoice at the sight."
Everywhere, everywhere, Christmas tonight.

PHILLIPS BROOKS (1835–1893) WAS AN AMERICAN PRIEST AND THEOLO-
GIAN. HE PUBLISHED SEVERAL VOLUMES OF SERMONS AND ALSO WROTE
THE CHRISTMAS CAROL "O LITTLE TOWN OF BETHLEHEM." HE IS
PERHAPS BEST KNOWN AS ABRAHAM LINCOLN'S PASTOR.

A Child Will Be Born

The people who walked in darkness
have seen a great light;
those who lived in a land of deep darkness—
on them light has shined. . . .
For a child has been born for us,
a son given to us;
authority rests upon his shoulders;
and he is named
Wonderful Counselor, Mighty God,
Everlasting Father, Prince of Peace.
His authority shall grow continually,
and there shall be endless peace
for the throne of David and his kingdom.
He will establish and uphold it
with justice and with righteousness
from this time onward and forevermore.
The zeal of the LORD of hosts will do this.

—Isaiah 9:2, 6–7

Advent Meditations

Pope John Paul II

My Christmas Prayer

Emmanuel! You are in our midst. *You are with us.* [You are] coming down to the uttermost consequences [of the Covenant] made from the beginning with man, and in spite of the fact that it was violated and broken so many times . . . you are with us! *Emmanuel!* In a way that really surpasses everything that man could have thought of you. You are with us as a *man*. You are wonderful, truly wonderful, O God, Creator and Lord of the universe. God with the Father Almighty! The Logos! The only Son! *God of power!* You are with us as man, as a *newborn* baby of the human race, *absolutely weak*, wrapped in swaddling clothes and placed in a manger, "because there was no place for them" in any inn (Luke 2:7). Is it not precisely that because you became man in this way, without a roof to shelter you, that you became *nearest to man?* Is it not precisely because you yourself, the newborn Jesus, are without a roof that you are nearest to those brothers and sisters . . . who *have lost their homes* through the terrible earthquakes and storms? And the people that really come to their aid are precisely the ones who have you in their hearts, you who were born at Bethlehem without a home.

CHRISTMAS DAY PRAYER AT THE VATICAN, 1980

41

In the Stable of Bethlehem

God is born and the powers tremble—the Lord of the heavens lies naked. The star fades and the brilliance turns to shadow—the Infinite accepts limitation. Despised—reclothed in glory, the mortal—the King of eternity." That extract from a Polish Christmas carol is, in my opinion, outstandingly expressive of the mystery of God incarnate. It is a mystery embracing contrasts: light and the darkness of night, God's infiniteness and man's limitations, glory and humiliation, immortality and mortality, divinity and human poverty. People who are brought face-to-face with the *mysterium fascinosum* (the fascinating mystery) of this holy Christmas night which makes all races one become conscious that what then happened was something immensely important, something without parallel in the history of mankind. The Nativity brings us within touching distance, so to speak, of our spiritual birth in God through grace. Born through faith and grace, we have been called *children of God;* and so we are says St. John (1 John 3:1).

SIGN OF CONTRADICTION

A Christmas Prayer

We thank you, eternal Father, for the Motherhood of the Virgin Mary, who under the protection of Joseph, the carpenter of Nazareth, brought your Son into the world, in utter poverty. "He came to his own home, and his own people received him not" (John 1:11). And yet, ye received all of us from his very birth and embraced each one of us with the eternal love of the Father, with the love that saves man, that raises the human conscience from sin. In him we have *reconciliation and the forgiveness of sins*. We thank you heavenly Father, for the child laid in a manger: in him "the goodness and loving-kindness of God our Savior appeared" (Titus 3:4). We thank you, eternal Father, for *this love*, which comes down *like a frail infant into the history of each human being*. We thank you, because, though he was rich, yet for our sake he became poor, so that by his poverty we might become rich (2 Cor. 8:9). . . . *Impel* individuals and peoples to break down the wall of selfishness, of arrogance and hate, in order to open themselves to fraternal respect for all human beings, near or far, because they are people, brothers and sisters in Christ. Induce all individuals to offer the help necessary for those in need, to renew their own hearts in the grace of Christ the Redeemer.

MESSAGE AT ST. PETER'S BASILICA, DECEMBER 25, 1983

The Lord Is Near

The liturgy of Advent reminds us every day that the Lord is near. This closeness of the Lord is felt by all of us: both by us priests, reciting every day the marvelous major antiphons and by all Christians who try to prepare their hearts and their consciences for his coming. I know that in this period the confessionals of churches in my country, Poland, are thronged (no less than during Lent). I think that is certainly the same in Italy also, and wherever a deep spirit of faith makes the need felt of opening one's soul to the Lord who is about to come. The greatest joy of this expectation of Advent is that felt by the children. I remember that it was just they who hurried most willingly in the parishes of my country to the Masses celebrated at dawn. The antiphon *"Rorate . . . ,"* from the word with which the liturgy opens: *"Rorate Coeli,"* (*Drop down dew, O ye heavens from above*; Isa. 45:8) *still rings*. Every day they counted how many "rungs" still remained on the "heavenly ladder," by which Jesus would descend to the earth, in order to be able to meet him at mid-night of Christmas in the crib of Bethlehem.

DISCOURSE AT THE VATICAN, DECEMBER 20, 1978

The Coming of the Son of Man Is the Beginning of Life

This truth (the narrative of the end of the world), although it is recalled also in the liturgy (of the season of Advent), . . . is not, however, the specific truth announced now and in the whole period of Advent. It is not the principal word of the gospel. What is then the principal word? . . . It is the coming of the Son of Man. The principal word of the gospel is not "passing away," "absence," but "the coming" and "the presence." It is not "death," but "life." The gospel is the good news, because it speaks the truth about life in the context of death. The coming of the Son of Man is the beginning of this life, and it is precisely Advent that speaks to us of this beginning. Advent, which answers the question: How must men live in the world with the prospect of death? How must man, who may lose his life in a flash, how must he live in this world, in order to meet the Son of Man whose coming is the beginning of the new life, the life more powerful than death?

DISCOURSE AT THE PARISH OF ST. LEONARD OF PORT MAURICE,

ACHILIA, ITALY, NOVEMBER 30, 1980

POPE JOHN PAUL II (1920–2005), BORN KAROL JOZEF WOJTYLA, WAS ELECTED TO THE PAPACY IN 1978, AN OFFICE HE SERVED FOR NEARLY TWENTY-SEVEN YEARS.

Love came down at Christmas;
Love all lovely, love divine;
Love was born at Christmas,
Star and angels gave the sign.

CHRISTINA ROSSETTI

Christmas 1943

Anton Gill

1988

Helen Lewis was a classically trained dancer in Czechoslovakia when she was deported by the Nazis in 1941 and sent to live in a camp town for Jews. Thus began her imprisonment in a series of work camps, where she narrowly escaped death by gas chambers and peritonitis, among other things. This is her story of one Christmas in a concentration camp.

In August I was selected for a transport to go to work at Stutthof. By then I was a member of a small group of girls who looked after each other, and although the rail journey north was unspeakable, our spirits were high—at least for the first day of it. We were leaving Auschwitz. Whatever awaited us had to be better.

Stutthof itself was a halfway house for us. We just waited there until work was allocated. We were sent to a labor camp satellite of Stutthof called Kochstädt. We traveled there by open train, and that was actually bliss. It may sound crazy, but just to feel the wind on your face, and see the countryside, was a pleasure beyond price.

Our work was to level ground for an airstrip. We were close to the Baltic, and the earth was composed of sand dunes. We had to work fast because the concrete-laying machinery was hot on our heels. We were equipped with shovels with which we loaded the sand on to open trucks. It was back-breaking. I found it bearable as long as the sun shone, but the heat made it worse for some of the other girls, who couldn't take it and fell ill. The SS didn't give us much water.

None of the 800 men and women at Kochstädt died at work because every second counted. Prisoners who couldn't make it were loaded on to lorries and taken to the gas chambers at Stutthof. The lorries brought fresh people back the same day as replacements. The work we were doing was of actual and urgent importance to the Germans, so we were always kept topped up to 800.

Life was not made any easier by the SS. There was an *Oberaufseherin* [a camp guard] called Emma. She was about 35, I should think. She greeted us when she first met us with the information that prior to Stutthof she had been at Riga, where she had personally been responsible for the deaths of several thousand Jewish children. That was so we'd be under no illusion about what sort of woman she was.

One evening at roll-call I happened to be standing next to a Hungarian girl who casually mentioned that she hoped it wouldn't last long because it would cut down their rehearsal time if it did. It transpired that Emma was keen on culture and had encouraged a group of prisoners to put a Christmas show together: music, poetry and dance. I thought they were mad to devote precious rest hours to rehearsing, but later when I had another conversation with the same girl, it turned out that they were weak on the dance side of their programme. They were trying to do *Coppélia*, and I rashly told her not only that I knew the ballet but that I was a trained dancer.

The next thing I knew was that I was summoned from my barrack to the barrack where they held their rehearsals. I cursed my big mouth, but when I arrived I found that the barrack was warm and well lit. It was a huge room, and different girls were rehearsing different things in various corners. I saw some half a dozen girls prancing around appallingly to an accordionist who was, sure enough, playing *Coppélia*. No one paid any attention to me, and I sat down, furious that I was losing sleeping time. I watched the dancers until I could stand it no more and then I stood up again and said to them: "You got me to this damned rehearsal; now, do you want me to show you what to do or not?" They were all Hungarian girls and a bit shy, but we soon got over that, bridging the language barrier with German and Czech and French, and I started to choreograph them; and while I was doing it, the old energies took hold of me and I really got to work and the thing began to get pushed into shape. I forgot where I was—and then I realized that everyone else had stopped and they were all watching us. So I told my girls to try the dance from the top again, and it still looked pretty awful, but it had shape. I was high. The girl on the accordion, who was very good, started to play a tango. "Dance!" she called to me. And I started improvising to the tango, right there, in my striped uniform; and I got completely carried away. The Hungarians loved it and they hugged me and kissed me and said, "You are a star! We have a big, big star in our midst!" And someone who worked in the kitchens rushed off and brought me back margarine and a slice of bread. I took the food back to my barracks and woke my friends to share it with them, and of course I wasn't exhausted any more; I was more alive than I had been in years.

The next day brought me back to reality harshly and suddenly. The tiredness caught up with me, and it had snowed on the site, and the work was hellish. I knew it was going badly with me, and our overseer that day was one of the most unpleasant SS-men. I could feel him watching me, and finally approaching. I will never forget his words: "*Du bist auch schon reif für Stutthof.* [You look just about ready for Stutthof.]" The death sentence. But nothing came of it, and my number wasn't called that evening at roll call. Instead, I was summoned to the rehearsals again. The others had told Emma that they had found a brilliant dancing star, and she should come and see! I remember she sat on a chair and they ran through the whole program for her—she sat like a block of wood, arms crossed, terrifying, with eyes like slits. They left me until last.

When I had finished, there was a dreadful silence, and during it she just stood up and walked out. And I thought, oh God, and everyone was terribly depressed. Emma was displeased. I was dismissed with none of my former glory.

I passed one of the worst nights of my life. Next morning, at roll-call, I was as usual asleep on my feet, vaguely listening to the usual announcements being made over the loudspeaker system, when suddenly I was wide awake—my number had been called.

I was not kept in suspense long. By order of the *Oberaufseherin*, who had clearly thought it beneath her dignity the night before to indulge in any public display of enthusiasm—or maybe she just acted tough for effect—I was excused all other duties to take charge of rehearsals full-time until the day of the performance. Which meant I would be warm and indoors. There would be little physical labour, and what there was would be enjoyable. I was given an extra soup ration. Because it was dry in the rehearsal barrack, I would be able to wash some of my clothes. The other performers had to go out and work during the day as usual, so rehearsals didn't start until 5pm; until then I was free to do as I chose—which meant resting and sleeping. It was like a holiday; the only thing that marred it was that the performance would just be for the SS, but even that objection was taken away. In the spirit of Christmas, the SS decided to let the whole camp see it. And Emma became very enthusiastic, and organized make-up and costumes.

When it came, the evening was a great success. I had prepared two dances to do myself—the tango and a slow waltz—and

everything else went like clockwork. Everyone applauded like
mad and Emma's face was wreathed in smiles—she was barely
recognizable, and as proud as Punch to be Little Miss Culture. In the
enthusiasm of the moment, she ordered goulash to be made for the
whole cast of 30—though when it came it was very hard to eat it with
770 hungry pairs of eyes watching you. Mind you, it wasn't so rich
that it would do us any harm, but it was warm, and there was a bit
of meat and potato swimming around in it. We had to earn it again
though, because Emma was so delighted that she ordered a New Year's
program. The entire cast was taken off work to knock it together in a
week. I shudder to think today what it looked like, but in the circum-
stances it was considered to be high art. Anyway, it too was thought
a great success and Emma once again was very pleased—a fact which
led to a horrible moment afterwards, for she decided that there would
be a post-performance party dance for the cast. We all danced with
each other, of course, but Emma danced, too. Of course she chose
her partners, and of course she chose me. And I danced with her. The
tango. The foxtrot. I can remember how I felt when she put her arms
around me . . . .

But I felt that I had turned a corner. I'd had three weeks indoors,
with extra soup, and I was that much stronger. I might even have
put on a bit of weight. Now that I had to go into the cold again,
I thought I could manage a while longer; but it didn't last long,
because the Russians were getting closer.

We were evacuated on the morning of 27 January. I would certainly not have survived what was to follow without the reprieve my knowledge of dancing had earned me. Dance saved my life.

ANTON GILL PUBLISHED *The Journey Back from Hell: Conversations with Concentration Camp Survivors* IN 1988 TO PRESERVE THE ORAL HISTORY OF HOLOCAUST SURVIVORS.

Support for the King

May he have dominion from sea to sea
and from the River to the ends of the earth. . . .

May all kings fall down before him,
all nations give him service. . . .

May his name endure forever,
his fame continue as long as the sun.
May nations be blessed in him;
may they pronounce him happy.

—PSALM 72: 8, 11, 17

Love

The baby in the manger was a message
of God's love. And each year, Christmas
finds us quicker to love friends, family,
and even total strangers.

*For God so loved the world that he gave
his only Son, so that everyone who
believes in him may not perish
but may have eternal life.*

—JOHN 3:16

Our Christmas Meditation

E. Stanley Jones

1942

A little boy stood before the picture of his absent father, and then turned to his mother and wistfully said, "I wish father would step out of the picture."

This little boy expressed the deepest yearning of the human heart. We who have gazed upon the picture of God in nature are grateful, but not satisfied. We want our Father to step out of the impersonal picture and meet us as a Person. "The Impersonal laid no hold on my heart," says Tulsi Das, the great poet of India. It never does, for the human heart is personal and wants a Personal response.

"Why won't principles do? Why do we need a personal God?" someone asks. Well, suppose you go to a child crying for its mother and say, "Don't cry, little child; I'm giving to you the principle of motherhood." Would the tears dry and the face light up? Hardly. The child would brush aside your principle of motherhood and cry for its mother. We all want, not a principle nor a picture, but a Person.

The Father *has* stepped out of the picture. The Word *has* become flesh. That is the meaning of Christmas. Jesus is Immanuel—God with us. He is the Personal Approach from the Unseen. We almost gasp as the Picture steps out of the frame. We did not dare dream God was like Christ. But He is. Just as I analyze chemically the tiny sunbeam and discover in it the chemical make-up of the vast sun, so I look at the character and life of Jesus, and I know what God's character is like. He is Christlike.

"You have an advantage," said Dr. Hu Shih, the father of the Renaissance Movement in China, "in that all the ideas in Christianity have become embodied in a Person." Yes, and the further advantage of our faith is this: The Christmas word must become flesh in me. I too must become the word made flesh. I must be a miniature Christmas.

The Christian spirit is the Christmas spirit, extended through the whole year. It is the attitude toward every person, the atmosphere of every act. ✧

E. STANLEY JONES (1884–1973) WAS A METHODIST MINISTER AND THEOLOGIAN PERHAPS BEST KNOWN FOR HIS HUMANITARIAN EFFORTS IN INDIA.

It is Christmas every time you
let God love others through you. Yes,
it is Christmas every time you smile at
your brother and offer him your hand.

MOTHER TERESA

The Nativity

Rudyard Kipling

1918

The Babe was laid in the Manger
Between the gentle kine—
All safe from cold and danger—
"But it was not so with mine,
(With mine! With mine!)
"Is it well with the child, is it well?"
The waiting mother prayed.
"For I know not how he fell,
And I know not where he is laid."

A Star stood forth in Heaven;
The Watchers ran to see
The Sign of the Promise given—
"But there comes no sign to me
(To me! To me!)
"My child died in the dark.
Is it well with the child, is it well?
There was none to tend him or mark,
And I know not how he fell."

The Cross was raised on high;
The Mother grieved beside—
"But the Mother saw Him die
And took Him when He died.
(He died! He died!)
"Seemly and undefiled
His burial-place was made—
Is it well, is it well with the child?
For I know not where he is laid."

On the dawning of Easter Day
Comes Mary Magdalene;
But the Stone was rolled away,
And the Body was not within—
(Within! Within!)
"Ah, who will answer my word?
The broken mother prayed.
"They have taken away my Lord,
And I know not where He is laid."

"The Star stands forth in Heaven.
The watchers watch in vain
For Sign of the Promise given
Of peace on Earth again—

(Again! Again!)
"But I know for Whom he fell"—
The steadfast mother smiled,
"Is it well with the child—is it well?
It is well—it is well with the child!"

RUDYARD KIPLING (1865–1935), AN ENGLISH AUTHOR AND POET,
FAMOUSLY PENNED 1894'S *The Jungle Book* AND MANY OTHER BOOKS
AND POEMS FOR CHILDREN.

I thank God for Christmas.
Would that it lasted all year.
For on Christmas Eve, and Christmas Day,
all the world is a better place, and men
and women are more lovable. Love itself seeps
into every heart, and miracles happen.

PETER MARSHALL

Mary

Thomas Merton

1961

The genuine significance of Catholic devotion to Mary is to be seen in light of the Incarnation itself. The Church cannot separate the Son and the Mother. Because the Church conceives of the Incarnation as God's descent into flesh and into time, and His great gift of Himself to His creatures, she also believes that the one who was closest to Him in this great mystery was the one who participated most perfectly in the gift. When a room is heated by an open fire, surely there is nothing strange in the fact that those who stand closest to the fireplace are the ones who are warmest. And when God comes into the world through the instrumentality of one of His servants, then there is nothing surprising about the fact that His chosen instrument should have the greatest and most intimate share in the divine gift.

Mary, who was empty of all egotism, free from all sin, was as pure as the glass of a very clean window that has no other function than to admit the light of the sun. If we rejoice in that light, we implicitly praise the cleanness of the window. And of course it might be argued that in such a case we might forget the window altogether. This is true. And yet the Son of God, in emptying

Himself of His majestic power, having become a child, abandoning Himself in complete dependence to the loving care of a human Mother, in a certain sense draws our attention once again to her. The Light has wished to remind us of the window, because He is grateful to her and because He has an infinitely tender and personal love for her. If He asks us to share this love, it is certainly a great grace and a privilege, and one of the most important aspects of this privilege is that it enables us to some extent to appreciate the mystery of God's great love and respect for His creatures.✧

THOMAS MERTON (1915–1968) WAS A TRAPPIST MONK WHO WROTE PROLIFICALLY ABOUT SPIRITUALITY. HE ALSO STRONGLY SUPPORTED THE NONVIOLENT CIVIL RIGHTS MOVEMENT OF THE 1960S.

The Wanderers Return

Washington Irving

1819

I t is a beautiful arrangement, also, derived from days of yore, that this festival, which commemorates the announcement of the religion of peace and love, has been made the season for gathering together of family connections, and drawing closer again those bands of kindred hearts which the cares and pleasures and sorrows of the world are continually operating to cast loose; of calling back the children of a family who have launched forth in life, and wandered widely asunder, once more to assemble about the paternal hearth, that rallying-place of the affections, there to grow young and loving again among the endearing mementoes of childhood.✧

WASHINGTON IRVING (1783–1859), AN AUTHOR AND ESSAYIST, WAS AMONG THE FIRST AMERICAN WRITERS TO RECEIVE ACCLAIM IN EUROPE AND PUBLISHED MANY ESSAYS AND NOVELS, INCLUDING "THE LEGEND OF SLEEPY HOLLOW" AND *Diedrich Knickerbocker's History of New York*. THE ABOVE SELECTION WAS INCLUDED IN AN INSTALLMENT OF IRVING'S *The Sketch Book*, A COLLECTION THAT ALSO INCLUDED "RIP VAN WINKLE."

JACK FROST

The Gift of the Magi

O. Henry

1905

One dollar and eighty-seven cents. That was all. And sixty cents of it was in pennies. Pennies saved one and two at a time by bulldozing the grocer and the vegetable man and the butcher until one's cheeks burned with the silent imputation of parsimony that such close dealing implied. Three times Della counted it. One dollar and eighty-seven cents. And the next day would be Christmas.

There was clearly nothing to do but flop down on the shabby little couch and howl. So Della did it. Which instigates the moral reflection that life is made up of sobs, sniffles, and smiles, with sniffles predominating.

While the mistress of the home is gradually subsiding from the first stage to the second, take a look at the home. A furnished flat at $8 per week. It did not exactly beggar description, but it certainly had that word on the lookout for the mendicancy squad.

In the vestibule below was a letter-box into which no letter would go, and an electric button from which no mortal finger could coax a ring. Also appertaining thereunto was a card bearing the name "Mr. James Dillingham Young."

The "Dillingham" had been flung to the breeze during a former period of prosperity when its possessor was being paid $30 per week. Now, when the income was shrunk to $20, though, they were thinking seriously of contracting to a modest and unassuming D. But whenever Mr. James Dillingham Young came home and reached his flat above he was called "Jim" and greatly hugged by Mrs. James Dillingham Young, already introduced to you as Della. Which is all very good.

Della finished her cry and attended to her cheeks with the powder rag. She stood by the window and looked out dully at a gray cat walking a gray fence in a gray backyard. Tomorrow would be Christmas Day, and she had only $1.87 with which to buy Jim a present. She had been saving every penny she could for months, with this result. Twenty dollars a week doesn't go far. Expenses had been greater than she had calculated. They always are. Only $1.87 to buy a present for Jim. Her Jim. Many a happy hour she had spent planning for something nice for him. Something fine and rare and sterling—something just a little bit near to being worthy of the honor of being owned by Jim.

There was a pier glass between the windows of the room. Perhaps you have seen a pier glass in an $8 flat. A very thin and very agile person may, by observing his reflection in a rapid sequence of longitudinal strips, obtain a fairly accurate conception of his looks. Della, being slender, had mastered the art.

Suddenly she whirled from the window and stood before the glass. Her eyes were shining brilliantly, but her face had lost its color within twenty seconds. Rapidly she pulled down her hair and let it fall to its full length.

Now, there were two possessions of the James Dillingham Youngs in which they both took a mighty pride. One was Jim's gold watch that had been his father's and his grandfather's. The other was Della's hair. Had the queen of Sheba lived in the flat across the airshaft, Della would have let her hair hang out the window some day to dry just to depreciate Her Majesty's jewels and gifts. Had King Solomon been the janitor, with all his treasures piled up in the basement, Jim would have pulled out his watch every time he passed, just to see him pluck at his beard from envy.

So now Della's beautiful hair fell about her rippling and shining like a cascade of brown waters. It reached below her knee and made itself almost a garment for her. And then she did it up again nervously and quickly. Once she faltered for a minute and stood still while a tear or two splashed on the worn red carpet.

On went her old brown jacket; on went her old brown hat. With a whirl of skirts and with the brilliant sparkle still in her eyes, she fluttered out the door and down the stairs to the street.

Where she stopped the sign read: "Mme. Sofronie. Hair Goods of All Kinds." One flight up Della ran, and collected herself, panting. Madame, large, too white, chilly, hardly looked the "Sofronie."

"Will you buy my hair?" asked Della.

"I buy hair," said Madame. "Take yer hat off and let's have a sight at the looks of it."

Down rippled the brown cascade.

"Twenty dollars," said Madame, lifting the mass with a practised hand.

"Give it to me quick," said Della.

Oh, and the next two hours tripped by on rosy wings. Forget the hashed metaphor. She was ransacking the stores for Jim's present.

She found it at last. It surely had been made for Jim and no one else. There was no other like it in any of the stores, and she had turned all of them inside out. It was a platinum fob chain simple and chaste in design, properly proclaiming its value by substance alone and not by meretricious ornamentation—as all good things should do. It was even worthy of The Watch. As soon as she saw it she knew that it must be Jim's. It was like him. Quietness and value—the description applied to both. Twenty-one dollars they took from her for it, and she hurried home with the 87 cents. With that chain on his watch Jim might be properly anxious about the time in any company. Grand as the watch was, he sometimes looked at it on the sly on account of the old leather strap that he used in place of a chain.

When Della reached home her intoxication gave way a little to prudence and reason. She got out her curling irons and lighted the gas and went to work repairing the ravages made by generosity added to love. Which is always a tremendous task, dear friends—a mammoth task.

Within forty minutes her head was covered with tiny, close-lying curls that made her look wonderfully like a truant schoolboy. She looked at her reflection in the mirror long, carefully, and critically.

"If Jim doesn't kill me," she said to herself, "before he takes a second look at me, he'll say I look like a Coney Island chorus girl. But what could I do—oh! what could I do with a dollar and eighty-seven cents?"

At 7 o'clock the coffee was made and the frying-pan was on the back of the stove hot and ready to cook the chops.

Jim was never late. Della doubled the fob chain in her hand and sat on the corner of the table near the door that he always entered. Then she heard his step on the stair away down on the first flight, and she turned white for just a moment. She had a habit of saying a little silent prayer about the simplest everyday things, and now she whispered: "Please God, make him think I am still pretty."

The door opened and Jim stepped in and closed it. He looked thin and very serious. Poor fellow, he was only twenty-two—and to be burdened with a family! He needed a new overcoat and he was without gloves.

Jim stopped inside the door, as immovable as a setter at the scent of quail. His eyes were fixed upon Della, and there was an expression in them that she could not read, and it terrified her. It was not anger, nor surprise, nor disapproval, nor horror, nor any of the sentiments that she had been prepared for. He simply stared at her fixedly with that peculiar expression on his face.

Della wriggled off the table and went for him.

"Jim, darling," she cried, "don't look at me that way. I had my hair cut off and sold because I couldn't have lived through Christmas without giving you a present. It'll grow out again—you won't mind, will you? I just had to do it. My hair grows awfully fast. Say 'Merry Christmas!' Jim, and let's be happy. You don't know what a nice—what a beautiful, nice gift I've got for you."

"You've cut off your hair?" asked Jim, laboriously, as if he had not arrived at that patent fact yet even after the hardest mental labor.

"Cut it off and sold it," said Della. "Don't you like me just as well, anyhow? I'm me without my hair, ain't I?"

Jim looked about the room curiously.

"You say your hair is gone?" he said, with an air almost of idiocy.

"You needn't look for it," said Della. "It's sold, I tell you—sold and gone, too. It's Christmas Eve, boy. Be good to me, for it went for you. Maybe the hairs of my head were numbered," she went on with sudden serious sweetness, "but nobody could ever count my love for you. Shall I put the chops on, Jim?"

Out of his trance Jim seemed quickly to wake. He enfolded his Della. For ten seconds let us regard with discreet scrutiny some inconsequential object in the other direction. Eight dollars a week or a million a year—what is the difference? A mathematician or a wit would give you the wrong answer. The magi brought valuable gifts, but that was not among them. This dark assertion will be illuminated later on.

Jim drew a package from his overcoat pocket and threw it upon the table.

"Don't make any mistake, Dell," he said, "about me. I don't think there's anything in the way of a haircut or a shave or a shampoo that could make me like my girl any less. But if you'll unwrap that package you may see why you had me going a while at first."

White fingers and nimble tore at the string and paper. And then an ecstatic scream of joy; and then, alas! a quick feminine change to hysterical tears and wails, necessitating the immediate employment of all the comforting powers of the lord of the flat.

For there lay The Combs—the set of combs, side and back, that Della had worshipped long in a Broadway window. Beautiful combs, pure tortoise shell, with jewelled rims—just the shade to wear in the beautiful vanished hair. They were expensive combs, she knew, and her heart had simply craved and yearned over them without the least hope of possession. And now, they were hers, but the tresses that should have adorned the coveted adornments were gone.

But she hugged them to her bosom, and at length she was able to look up with dim eyes and a smile and say: "My hair grows so fast, Jim!"

And then Della leaped up like a little singed cat and cried, "Oh, oh!"

Jim had not yet seen his beautiful present. She held it out to him eagerly upon her open palm. The dull precious metal seemed to flash with a reflection of her bright and ardent spirit.

"Isn't it a dandy, Jim? I hunted all over town to find it. You'll have to look at the time a hundred times a day now. Give me your watch. I want to see how it looks on it."

Instead of obeying, Jim tumbled down on the couch and put his hands under the back of his head and smiled.

"Dell," said he, "let's put our Christmas presents away and keep 'em a while. They're too nice to use just at present. I sold the watch to get the money to buy your combs. And now suppose you put the chops on."

The magi, as you know, were wise men—wonderfully wise men—who brought gifts to the Babe in the manger. They invented the art of giving Christmas presents. Being wise, their gifts were no doubt wise ones, possibly bearing the privilege of exchange in case of duplication. And here I have lamely related to you the uneventful chronicle of two foolish children in a flat who most unwisely sacrificed for each other the greatest treasures of their house. But in a last word to the wise of these days let it be said that of all who give gifts these two were the wisest. Of all who give and receive gifts, such as they are wisest. Everywhere they are wisest. They are the magi.✧

O. HENRY (1862–1910), BORN WILLIAM SYDNEY PORTER, PUBLISHED MANY SHORT STORIES AT THE TURN OF THE TWENTIETH CENTURY, MOST COMMONLY ABOUT THE LIVES OF NEW YORK CITY RESIDENTS.

Christmas Day in the Morning

Pearl S. Buck

1955

He woke suddenly and completely. It was four o'clock, the hour at which his father had always called him to get up and help with the milking. Strange how the habits of his youth clung to him still! Fifty years ago, and his father had been dead for thirty years, and yet he waked at four o'clock in the morning. He had trained himself to turn over and go to sleep, but this morning, because it was Christmas, he did not try to sleep.

Yet what was the magic of Christmas now? His childhood and youth were long past, and his own children had grown up and gone. Some of them lived only a few miles away, but they had their own families, and though they would come in as usual toward the end of the day, they had explained with infinite gentleness that they wanted their children to build Christmas memories about their houses, not his. He was left alone with his wife.

Yesterday she had said, "It isn't worthwhile, perhaps—"

And he had said, "Oh, yes, Alice, even if there are only the two of us, let's have a Christmas of our own."

Then she had said, "Let's not trim the tree until tomorrow, Robert—just so it's ready when the children come. I'm tired."

He had agreed, and the tree was still out in the back entry.

He lay in his big bed in his room. The door to her room was shut because she was a light sleeper, and sometimes he had restless nights. Years ago they had decided to use separate rooms. It meant nothing, they said, except neither of them slept as well as they once had. They had been married so long that nothing could separate them, actually.

Why did he feel so awake tonight? For it was still night, a clear and starry night. No moon, of course, but the stars were extraordinary!

Now that he thought of it, the stars seemed always large and clear before the dawn of Christmas Day. There was one star now that was certainly larger and brighter than any of the others. He could even imagine it moving, as it had seemed to him to move one night long ago.

He slipped back in time, as he did so easily nowadays. He was fifteen years old and still on his father's farm. He loved his father. He had not known it until one day a few days before Christmas, when he had overheard what his father was saying to his mother.

"Mary, I hate to call Rob in the mornings. He's growing so fast and he needs his sleep. If you could see how he sleeps when I go in to wake him up! I wish I could manage alone."

"Well, you can't, Adam." His mother's voice was brisk. "Besides, he isn't a child anymore. It's time he took his turn."

"Yes," his father said slowly. "But I sure do hate to wake him."

When he heard these words, something in him spoke: his father loved him! He had never thought of that before, taking for granted the tie of their blood. Neither his father nor his mother talked about loving their children—they had no time for such things. There was always so much to do on the farm.

Now that he knew his father loved him, there would be no loitering in the mornings and having to be called again. He got up after that, stumbling blindly in his sleep, and pulled on his clothes, his eyes tight shut. But he got up.

And then on the night before Christmas, that year when he was fifteen, he lay for a few minutes thinking about the next day. They were poor, and most of the excitement was in the turkey they had raised themselves and mince pies his mother made. His sisters sewed presents and his mother and father always bought him something he needed, not only a warm jacket, maybe, but something more, such as a book. And he saved and bought them each something, too.

He wished, that Christmas when he was fifteen, he had a better present for his father. As usual he had gone to the ten-cent store and bought a tie. It had seemed nice enough until he lay thinking the night before Christmas, and then he wished that he had heard his father and mother talking in time for him to save for something better.

He lay on his side, his head supported by his elbow, and looked out of his attic window. The stars were bright, much brighter than he ever remembered seeing them, and one star in particular was so bright that he wondered if it were really the Star of Bethlehem.

"Dad," he had once asked when he was a little boy, "What is a stable?"

"It's just a barn," his father had replied, "like ours."

Then Jesus had been born in a barn, and to a barn the shepherds and the Wise Men had come, bringing their Christmas gifts!

The thought struck him like a silver dagger. Why should he not give his father a special gift too, out there in the barn? He could get up early, earlier than four o'clock, and he could creep into the barn and get all the milking done. He'd do it alone, milk and clean up, and then when his father went in to start the milking he'd see it all done. And he would know who had done it.

He laughed to himself as he gazed at the stars. It was what he would do, and he mustn't sleep too sound.

He must have waked twenty times, scratching a match to look each time to look at his old watch—midnight, and half past one, and then two o'clock.

At a quarter to three he got up and put on his clothes. He crept downstairs, careful of the creaky boards, and let himself out. The cows looked at him, sleepy and surprised. It was early for them, too.

"So, boss," he whispered. They accepted him placidly, and he fetched some hay for each cow and then got the milking pail and the big milk cans.

He had never milked all alone before, but it seemed almost easy. He kept thinking about his father's surprise. His father would come in and get him, saying that he would get things started while Rob was getting dressed. He'd go to the barn, open the door, and then he'd go get the two big empty milk cans. But they wouldn't be waiting or empty, they'd be standing in the milk-house, filled.

"What the—," he could hear his father exclaiming.

He smiled and milked steadily, two strong streams rushing into the pail, frothing and fragrant.

The task went more easily than he had ever known it to go before. Milking for once was not a chore. It was something else, a gift to his father who loved him. He finished, the two milk cans were full, and he covered them and closed the milk-house door carefully, making sure of the latch.

Back in his room he had only a minute to pull off his clothes in the darkness and jump into bed, for he heard his father up. He put the covers over his head to silence his quick breathing. The door opened.

"Rob!" His father called. "We have to get up, son, even if it is Christmas."

"Aw-right," he said sleepily.

"I'll go on out," his father said. "I'll get things started."

The door closed and he lay still, laughing to himself. In just a few minutes his father would know. His dancing heart was ready to jump from his body.

"Rob!"

"Yes, Dad—"

His father was laughing, a queer sobbing sort of laugh. "Thought you'd fool me, did you?"

His father was standing by his bed, feeling for him, pulling away the cover.

"It's for Christmas, Dad!"

He found his father and clutched him in a great hug. He felt his father's arms go around him. It was dark and they could not see each other's faces.

"Son, I thank you. Nobody ever did a nicer thing—"

"Oh, Dad, I want you to know—I do want to by good!" The words broke from him of their own will. He did not know what to say. His heart was bursting with love.

"Well, I reckon I can go back to bed and sleep," his father said after a moment. "No, hark—the little ones are waked up. Come to think of it, son, I've never seen you children when you first saw the Christmas tree. I was always in the barn. Come on!"

He got up and pulled on his clothes again and they went down to the Christmas tree, and soon the sun was creeping up to where the star had been. Oh, what a Christmas, and how his heart had nearly burst again with shyness and pride as his father told his mother and made the younger children listen about how he, Rob, had got up all by himself.

"The best Christmas gift I ever had, and I'll remember it, son, every year on Christmas morning, so long as I live."

They had both remembered it, and now that his father was dead, he remembered it alone: that blessed Christmas dawn when, alone with the cows in the barn, he had made his first gift of true love.

This Christmas he wanted to write a card to his wife and tell her how much he loved her, it had been a long time since he had really told her, although he loved her in a very special way, much more than he ever had when they were young. He had been fortunate that she had loved him. Ah, that was the true joy of life, the ability to love. Love was still alive in him, it still was.

It occurred to him suddenly that it was alive because long ago it had been born in him when he knew his father loved him. That was it: Love alone could awaken love. And he could give the gift again and again. This morning, this blessed Christmas morning, he would give it to his beloved wife. He could write it down in a letter for her to read and keep forever.

He went to his desk and began his love letter to his wife: My dearest love . . .

Such a happy, happy Christmas!✧

PEARL S. BUCK (1892–1973) AUTHORED MORE THAN SEVENTY BOOKS, INCLUDING THE PULITZER PRIZE-WINNING *The Good Earth*. IN 1938, SHE BECAME THE FIRST AMERICAN WOMAN TO WIN THE NOBEL PRIZE IN LITERATURE.

Peace

The angels spoke peace to the shepherds
in the field. And even today, as Christmas
approaches, we find ourselves reaching
for goodwill for all.

*Glory to God in the highest heaven,
and on earth peace among those whom he favors!*

—Luke 2:14

Christmas

Frederick Buechner

2004

The lovely old carols played and replayed till their effect is like a dentist's drill or jackhammer, the bathetic banalities of the pulpit and the chilling commercialism of almost everything else, people spending money they can't afford on presents you neither need nor want, "Rudolph the Red-Nosed Reindeer," the plastic tree, the cornball crèche, the Hallmark Virgin. Yet for all our efforts, we've never quite managed to ruin it. That in itself is part of the miracle, a part you can see. Most of the miracles you can't see, or don't.

The young clergyman and his wife do all the things you do on Christmas Eve. They string the lights and hang the ornaments. They supervise the hanging of the stockings. They tuck in the children. They lug the presents down out of hiding and pile them under the tree. Just as they're about to fall exhausted into bed, the husband remembers his neighbor's sheep. The man asked him to feed them for him while he was away, and in the press of other matters that night he forgot all about them. So down the hill he goes through the knee-deep snow. He gets two bales of hay from the barn and carries them out to the shed. There's a forty-watt bulb hanging by its cord from the low roof, and he turns it on. The sheep huddle in a corner watching as he snaps the baling twine, shakes the squares of hay apart, and starts scattering it. Then they come bumbling and shoving to get at it with their foolish, mild faces, the puffs of their breath showing in the air. He is reaching to turn off the bulb and leave when suddenly he realizes where he is. The winter darkness. The glimmer of light. The smell of the hay and the sound of the animals eating. Where he is, of course, is the manger.

He only just saw it. He whose business it is above everything else to have an eye for such things is all but blind in that eye. He who on his best days believes that everything that is most precious anywhere comes from that manger might easily have gone home to bed never knowing that he had himself just been in the manger. The world is the manger. It is only by grace that he happens to see this other part of the miracle.

Christmas itself is by grace. It could never have survived our own blindness and depredations otherwise. It could never have *happened* otherwise. Perhaps it is the very wildness and strangeness of the grace that has led us to try to tame it. We have reduced it to an occasion we feel at home with, at best a touching and beautiful occasion, at worst a trite and cloying one. But if the Christmas event in itself is indeed—as a matter of cold, hard fact—all it's cracked up to be, then even at best our efforts are misleading.

The Word became flesh. Ultimate Mystery born with a skull you could crush one-handed. Incarnation. It is not tame. It is not touching. It is not beautiful. It is uninhabitable terror. It is unthinkable darkness riven with unbearable light. Agonized laboring led to it, vast upheavals of intergalactic space/time split apart, a wrenching and tearing of the very sinews of reality itself. You can only cover your eyes and shudder before it, before *this*: "God of God, Light of Light, very God of very God . . . who for us and for our salvation," as the Nicene Creed puts it, "came down from heaven."

Came down. Only then do we dare uncover our eyes and see what we can see. It is the Resurrection and the Life she holds in her arms. It is the bitterness of death he takes at her breast. ✧

FREDERICK BUECHNER (1926–), A PRESBYTERIAN MINISTER AND THEOLOGIAN, HAS MORE THAN THIRTY PUBLISHED BOOKS IN A BROAD RANGE OF GENRES AND TOPICS. HE IS CONSIDERED ONE OF THE MOST WIDELY READ CONTEMPORARY AUTHORS AMONG CHRISTIAN AUDIENCES, AND IS A CHERISHED VOICE ON SPIRITUALITY AND CHRISTIAN LIVING.

This is the month, and this the happy morn,
Wherein the Son of Heaven's eternal King,
Of wedded Maid and Virgin Mother born,
Our great redemption from above did bring;
For so the holy sages once did sing,
That he our deadly forfeit should release,
And with his Father work us a perpetual peace.

JOHN MILTON

Jesus Brings the Priceless Gift of Peace to All

Pope John Paul II

The *season of Advent* begins the journey of spiritual renewal in preparation for Christmas. The voices of the prophets who proclaim the Messiah ring out in the liturgy, asking for conversion of heart and for prayer. John the Baptist, the last of these and the greatest, cries out, *"Prepare the way of the Lord!"* (Luke 3:4), because he "will come to visit his people in peace" (Isa. 9:6). Come Christ, Prince of Peace! Preparing for his birth means reawakening the hope of peace in ourselves and throughout the world. *Build peace in hearts first of all* by laying down the weapons of rancor, revenge, and every form of selfishness. The world cries out for peace! I am thinking especially with deep sorrow of the latest episodes of violence in the Middle East and on the African continent, as well as those that daily newspapers are recording in so many other parts of the globe. I renew my appeal to the leaders of the great religions: let us join forces in preaching nonviolence, forgiveness, and reconciliation! *"Blessed are the meek, for they shall inherit the earth"* (Matt. 5:5). In this journey of expectation and hope that is Advent, the ecclesial community is identified more closely than ever with the Most Holy Virgin. May it be she, the Virgin of expectation, who helps us to open our hearts to the One who, by his coming among us, brings the priceless gift of peace to all humanity.

Discourse at the Vatican, December 3, 2003

A Christmas Blessing

Andrew M. Greeley

2001

May the Christmas light glow in your window as you come home on a dark and stormy night.

May the music of carols warm your discouraged souls and make you want to sing again.

May the crib scene catch your eye and hold you in its fascination.

May you realize that every gift is as special as you want to make it.

May the Christmas tree draw you to its dazzling lights.

May your love be even more dazzling and welcome everyone home.

May Jesus and Mary and Joseph bless you and all yours and keep you patient and happy and joyous all the season long.

May you remember as best you can the poor and the sick and lonely and the hungry and the frightened.

And may it be, no matter what, the best Christmas ever.

Amen.✧

ANDREW GREELEY (1928–), HAS SERVED AS A CATHOLIC PRIEST AND SOCIOLOGY PROFESSOR, AND HAS ALSO BEEN A POPULAR NOVELIST AND *Chicago Sun-Times* COLUMNIST.

Christmas When I Was Sixteen

Laura Ingalls Wilder

December 1924

The snow was scudding low over the drifts of the white world outside the little claim shanty. It was blowing through the cracks in its walls and forming little piles and miniature drifts on the floor, and even on the desks before which several children sat, trying to study; for this abandoned claim shanty, which had served as the summer home of a homesteader on the Dakota prairie, was being used as a schoolhouse during the winter.

The walls were made of one thickness of wide boards with cracks between and the enormous stove that stood nearly in the center of the one room could scarcely keep out the frost, thought its sides were a glowing red. The children were dressed warmly and had been allowed to gather closely around the stove following the advice of the county superintendent of schools who, on a recent visit, had said that the only thing he had to say to them was to keep their feet warm.

This was my first school; I'll not say how many years ago, but I was only sixteen years old and twelve miles from home during a frontier winter. I walked a mile over the unbroken snow from my boarding place to school every morning and back at night. There were only a few pupils, and on this particular snowy afternoon, they were restless, for it was nearing 4 o'clock and tomorrow was Christmas. "Teacher" was restless too though she tried not to show it, for she was wondering if she could get home for Christmas Day.

It was almost too cold to hope for Father to come, and a storm was hanging in the northwest which might mean a blizzard at any minute. Still, tomorrow was Christmas—and then there was a jingle of sleigh bells outside. A man in a huge fur coat in a sleigh full of robes passed the window. I was going home after all!

When one thinks of twelve miles now, it is in terms of motor cars and means only a few minutes. It was different then, and I'll never forget that ride. The bells made a merry jingle, and the fur robes were warm; but the weather was growing colder, and the snow was drifting so that the horses must break their way through the drifts.

We were facing the strong wind, and every little while he, who later became the "Man of the Place," must stop the team, get out in the snow, and by putting his hands over each horse's nose in turn, thaw the ice from them where the breath had frozen over their nostrils. Then he would get back in the sleigh, and on we'd go until once more the horses could not breathe for the ice.

When we reached the journey's end, it was 40 degrees below zero; the snow was blowing so thickly that we could not see across the street; and I was so chilled that I had to be half carried into the house. But I was home for Christmas, and cold and danger were forgotten.

Such magic there is in Christmas to draw the absent ones home, and if unable to go in the body, the thoughts will hover there! Our hearts grow tender with childhood memories and love of kindred, and we are better throughout the year for having, in spirit, become a child again at Christmastime.✧

LAURA INGALLS WILDER (1867–1957) BEGAN WRITING THE *LITTLE HOUSE* BOOK SERIES IN 1932. THE BOOKS CONTINUE TO BE READ AS ICONIC TALES OF LIFE ON THE PRAIRIE.

He came, not as a flash of light or as an unapproachable conqueror, but as one whose first cries were heard by a peasant girl and a sleepy carpenter. God tapped humanity on its collective shoulder, "Pardon me," he said, and eternity interrupted time, divinity interrupted carnality, and heaven interrupted the earth in the form of a baby. Christianity was born in one big heavenly interruption.

MAX LUCADO

Hark! The Herald Angels Sing

Charles Wesley

1739

Hark! the herald angels sing
"Glory to the newborn King!
Peace on earth and mercy mild
God and sinners reconciled!"
Joyful, all ye nations rise
Join the triumph of the skies
With the angelic host proclaim:
"Christ is born in Bethlehem!"
Hark! the herald angels sing
"Glory to the newborn King!"

Christ by highest heav'n adored
Christ the everlasting Lord!
Late in time behold Him come
Offspring of a Virgin's womb.
Veiled in flesh the Godhead see;
Hail the incarnate Deity,

Pleased as man with man to dwell,

Jesus, our Emmanuel

Hark! the herald angels sing

"Glory to the newborn King!"

Hail the heav'n-born Prince of Peace!

Hail the Son of Righteousness!

Light and life to all He brings,

Ris'n with healing in His wings.

Mild He lays His glory by,

Born that man no more may die,

Born to raise the sons of earth,

Born to give them second birth.

Hark! The herald angels sing

"Glory to the newborn King!"

CHARLES WESLEY (1707–1788) WAS THE BROTHER OF JOHN WESLEY, THE FOUNDER OF METHODISM. HE WROTE MANY POEMS AND HYMNS. "HARK THE HERALD ANGELS SING" WAS SET TO MUSIC MORE THAN ONE HUNDRED YEARS AFTER WESLEY WROTE IT AND BECAME THE CHRISTMAS CAROL WE KNOW AND LOVE TODAY.

Holiday and Holy Day, Christmas is more than a Yule log, holly, or a tree. It is more than natural good cheer and the giving of gifts. Christmas is even more than the feast of the home and of children, the feast of love and friendship. It is more than all these together. Christmas is Christ, the Christ of justice and charity, of freedom and peace.

FRANCIS CARDINAL SPELLMAN

Christmas Bells

Henry Wadsworth Longfellow

1863

I heard the bells on Christmas Day
Their old, familiar carols play,
And wild and sweet
The words repeat
Of peace on earth, good-will to men!

And thought how, as the day had come,
The belfries of all Christendom
Had rolled along
The unbroken song
Of peace on earth, good-will to men!

Till, ringing, singing on its way
The world revolved from night to day,
A voice, a chime,
A chant sublime
Of peace on earth, good-will to men!

Then from each black, accursed mouth
The cannon thundered in the South,

And with the sound
The Carols drowned
Of peace on earth, good-will to men!

And in despair I bowed my head;
'There is no peace on earth,' I said;
'For hate is strong,
And mocks the song
Of peace on earth, good-will to men!'

Then pealed the bells more loud and deep:
'God is not dead; nor doth he sleep!
The Wrong shall fail,
The Right prevail,
With peace on earth, good-will to men!'

HENRY WADSWORTH LONGFELLOW (1807–1882) WAS A WELL-KNOWN
PROFESSOR AND POET AND A MEMBER OF THE FIRESIDE POETS, A GROUP
THAT ALSO INCLUDED JOHN GREENLEAF WHITTIER AND OLIVER WENDELL
HOLMES. HE WROTE THIS POEM ONE CHRISTMAS AS HE NURSED HIS SON,
WHO HAD BEEN CRITICALLY INJURED IN THE CIVIL WAR.

Journey

Part of the classic Christmas story is the journey—
Mary and Joseph traveled to Bethlehem; the wise
men traveled from afar; the shepherds came into the
city. A journey brings inevitable challenges. But
it also brings rich rewards.

*Wise men from the East came to Jerusalem,
asking, "Where is the child who has been born
king of the Jews? For we observed his star at its
rising, and have come to pay him homage."*

—MATTHEW 2:1–2

The Other Wise Man

Henry Van Dyke

1896

In the days when Augustus Caesar was master of many kings and Herod reigned in Jerusalem, there lived in the city of Ecbatana, among the mountains of Persia, a certain man named Artaban. His house stood close to the outermost of the walls which encircled the royal treasury. From his roof he could look over the seven-fold battlements of black and white and crimson and blue and red and silver and gold, to the hill where the summer palace of the Parthian emperors glittered like a jewel in a crown.

. . . High above the trees a dim glow of light shone through the curtained arches of the upper chamber, where the master of the house was holding council with his friends. . . .

"Welcome!" he said, in his low, pleasant voice, as one after another entered the room—"welcome, Abdus; peace be with you, Rhodaspes and Tigranes, and with you my father, Abgarus. You are all welcome. This house grows bright with the joy of your presence."

There were nine of the men, differing widely in age, but alike in the richness of their dress of many-coloured silks, and in the massive golden collars around their necks, marking them as

Parthian nobles, and in the winged circles of gold resting upon their breasts, the sign of the followers of Zoroaster.

They took their places around a small black altar at the end of the room, where a tiny flame was burning. . . . "You have come to-night," said [Artaban], looking around the circle, "at my call, as the faithful scholars of Zoroaster, to renew your worship and rekindle your faith in the God of Purity, even as this fire has been rekindled on the altar. We worship not the fire, but Him of whom it is the chosen symbol, because it is the purest of all created things. It speaks to us of one who is Light and Truth. Is it not so, my father?"

"It is well said, my son," answered the venerable Abgarus. "The enlightened are never idolaters. They lift the veil of form and go in to the shrine of reality, and new light and truth are coming to them continually through the old symbols." "Hear me, then, my father and my friends," said Artaban, "while I tell you of the new light and truth that have come to me through the most ancient of all signs. . . . Do not our own books tell us that this will come to pass, and that men will see the brightness of a great light?"

"That is true," said the voice of Abgarus; "every faithful disciple of Zoroaster knows the prophecy of the Avesta, and carries the word in his heart. 'In that day Sosiosh the Victorious shall arise out of the number of the prophets in the east country. Around him shall shine a mighty brightness, and he shall make life everlasting, incorruptible, and immortal, and the dead shall rise again.'"

. . . Artaban turned to Abgarus with a glow on his face, and said:

"My father, I have kept this prophecy in the secret place of my soul. Religion without a great hope would be like an altar without a living fire. And now the flame has burned more brightly, and by the light of it I have read other words which also have come from the fountain of Truth, and speak yet more clearly of the rising of the Victorious One in his brightness."

He drew from the breast of his tunic two small rolls of fine parchment, with writing upon them, and unfolded them carefully upon his knee.

"In the years that are lost in the past, long before our fathers came into the land of Babylon, there were wise men in Chaldea, from whom the first of the Magi learned the secret of the heavens. And of these Balaam the son of Beor was one of the mightiest. Hear the words of his prophecy: 'There shall come a star out of Jacob, and a sceptre shall arise out of Israel.'"

The lips of Tigranes drew downward with contempt, as he said:

"Judah was a captive by the waters of Babylon, and the sons of Jacob were in bondage to our kings. The tribes of Israel are scattered through the mountains like lost sheep, and from the remnant that dwells in Judea under the yoke of Rome neither star nor sceptre shall arise."

"And yet," answered Artaban, "it was the Hebrew Daniel, the mighty searcher of dreams, the counsellor of kings, the wise Belteshazzar, who was most honoured and beloved of our great King Cyrus. A prophet of sure things and a reader of the thoughts of the Eternal, Daniel proved himself to our people. And these are the words that he wrote." (Artaban read from the second roll:) "'Know, therefore, and understand that from the going forth of the commandment to restore Jerusalem, unto the Anointed One, the Prince, the time shall be seven and threescore and two weeks.'"

"But, my son," said Abgarus, doubtfully, "these are mystical numbers. Who can interpret them, or who can find the key that shall unlock their meaning?"

Artaban answered: "It has been shown to me and to my three companions among the Magi—Caspar, Melchior, and Balthazar. We have searched the ancient tablets of Chaldea and computed the time. It falls in this year. We have studied the sky, and in the spring of the year we saw two of the greatest planets draw near together in the sign of the Fish, which is the house of the Hebrews. We also saw a new star there, which shone for one night and then vanished. Now again the two great planets are meeting. This night is their conjunction. My three brothers are watching by the ancient Temple of the Seven Spheres, at Borsippa, in Babylonia, and I am watching here. If the star shines again, they will wait ten days for me at the temple, and then we will set out together for Jerusalem, to see and worship the promised one who shall be born King of Israel. I believe the sign will come. I have made ready for the journey. I have sold my possessions, and bought these three jewels—a sapphire, a ruby, and a pearl—to carry them as tribute to the King. And I ask you to go with me on the pilgrimage, that we may have joy together in finding the Prince who is worthy to be served."

. . . But his friends looked on with strange and alien eyes. A veil of doubt and mistrust came over their faces, like a fog creeping up from the marshes to hide the hills. They glanced at each other with looks of wonder and pity, as those who have listened to incredible sayings, the story of a wild vision, or the proposal of an impossible enterprise.

At last Tigranes said: "Artaban, this is a vain dream. It comes from too much looking upon the stars and the cherishing of lofty thoughts. It would be wiser to spend the time in gathering money for the new fire-temple at Chala. No king will ever rise from the broken race of Israel, and no end will ever come to the eternal strife of light and darkness. He who looks for it is a chaser of shadows. Farewell."

. . . One by one, they left the house of Artaban. . . . Then Abgarus went out of the azure chamber with its silver stars, and Artaban was left in solitude.

He gathered up the jewels and replaced them in his girdle. For a long time he stood and watched the flame that flickered and sank upon the altar. Then he crossed the hall, lifted the heavy curtain, and passed out between the pillars of porphyry to the terrace on the roof. . . .

Far over the eastern plain a white mist stretched like a lake. But where the distant peaks of Zagros serrated the western horizon the sky was clear. Jupiter and Saturn rolled together like drops of lambent flame about to blend in one.

As Artaban watched them, a steel-blue spark was born out of the darkness beneath, rounding itself with purple splendours to a crimson sphere, and spiring upward through rays of saffron and orange into a point of white radiance. Tiny and infinitely remote, yet perfect in every part, it pulsated in the enormous vault as if the three jewels in the Magian's girdle had mingled and been transformed into a living heart of light.

He bowed his head. He covered his brow with his hands.

"It is the sign," he said. "The King is coming, and I will go to meet him."

All night long, Vasda, the swiftest of Artaban's horses, had been waiting, saddled and bridled, in her stall, pawing the ground impatiently, and shaking her bit as if she shared the eagerness of her master's purpose, though she knew not its meaning. . . .

Artaban must indeed ride wisely and well if he would keep the appointed hour with the other Magi; for the route was a hundred and fifty parasangs, and fifteen was the utmost that he could travel in a day. But he knew Vasda's strength, and pushed forward without anxiety, making the fixed distance every day, though he must travel late into the night, and in the morning long before sunrise. . . . Artaban pressed onward until he arrived, at nightfall on the tenth day, beneath the shattered walls of populous Babylon.

Vasda was almost spent, and Artaban would gladly have turned into the city to find rest and refreshment for himself and for her. But he knew that it was three hours' journey yet to the Temple of the Seven Spheres, and he must reach the place by midnight if he would find his comrades waiting. So he did not halt, but rode steadily across the stubble-fields.

A grove of date-palms made an island of gloom in the pale yellow sea. As she passed into the shadow Vasda slackened her pace, and began to pick her way more carefully.

Near the farther end of the darkness an access of caution seemed to fall upon her. She scented some danger or difficulty; it was not in her heart to fly from it—only to be prepared for it, and to meet it wisely, as a good horse should do. The grove was close and silent as the tomb; not a leaf rustled, not a bird sang.

She felt her steps before her delicately, carrying her head low, and sighing now and then with apprehension. At last she gave a quick breath of anxiety and dismay, and stood stock-still, quivering in every muscle, before a dark object in the shadow of the last palm-tree.

Artaban dismounted. The dim starlight revealed the form of a man lying across the road. His humble dress and the outline of his haggard face showed that he was probably one of the Hebrews who still dwelt in great numbers around the city. His pallid skin, dry and yellow as parchment, bore the mark of the deadly fever which ravaged the marsh-lands in autumn. The chill of death was in his lean hand, and, as Artaban released it, the arm fell back inertly upon the motionless breast.

He turned away with a thought of pity, leaving the body to that strange burial which the Magians deemed most fitting—the funeral of the desert, from which the kites and vultures rise on dark wings, and the beasts of prey slink furtively away. When they are gone there is only a heap of white bones on the sand.

But, as he turned, a long, faint, ghostly sigh came from the man's lips. The bony fingers gripped the hem of the Magian's robe and held him fast.

Artaban's heart leaped to his throat, not with fear, but with a dumb resentment at the importunity of this blind delay.

How could he stay here in the darkness to minister to a dying stranger? What claim had this unknown fragment of human life upon his compassion or his service? If he lingered but for an hour he could hardly reach Borsippa at the appointed time. His companions would think he had given up the journey. They would go without him. He would lose his quest.

But if he went on now, the man would surely die. If Artaban stayed, life might be restored. His spirit throbbed and fluttered with the urgency of the crisis. Should he risk the great reward of his faith for the sake of a single deed of charity? Should he turn aside, if only for a moment, from the following of the star, to give a cup of cold water to a poor, perishing Hebrew?

"God of truth and purity," he prayed, "direct me in the holy path, the way of wisdom which Thou only knowest."

Then he turned back to the sick man. Loosening the grasp of his hand, he carried him to a little mound at the foot of the palm-tree.

He unbound the thick folds of the turban and opened the garment above the sunken breast. He brought water from one of the small canals near by, and moistened the sufferer's brow and mouth. He mingled a draught of one of those simple but potent remedies which he carried always in his girdle—for the Magians were physicians as well as astrologers—and poured it slowly between the colourless lips. Hour after hour he laboured as only a skilful healer of disease can do. At last the man's strength returned; he sat up and looked about him.

"Who art thou?" he said, in the rude dialect of the country, "and why hast thou sought me here to bring back my life?"

"I am Artaban the Magian, of the city of Ecbatana, and I am going to Jerusalem in search of one who is to be born King of the Jews, a great Prince and Deliverer of all men. I dare not delay any longer upon my journey, for the caravan that has waited for me may depart without me. But see, here is all that I have left of bread and wine, and here is a potion of healing herbs. When thy strength is restored thou canst find the dwellings of the Hebrews among the houses of Babylon."

The Jew raised his trembling hand solemnly to heaven.

"Now may the God of Abraham and Isaac and Jacob bless and prosper the journey of the merciful, and bring him in peace to his desired haven. Stay! I have nothing to give thee in return—only this: that I can tell thee where the Messiah must be sought. For our prophets have said that he should be born not in Jerusalem, but in Bethlehem of Judah. May the Lord bring thee in safety to that place, because thou hast had pity upon the sick."

It was already long past midnight. Artaban rode in haste, and Vasda, restored by the brief rest, ran eagerly through the silent plain and swam the channels of the river. She put forth the remnant of her strength, and fled over the ground like a gazelle.

But the first beam of the rising sun sent a long shadow before her as she entered upon the final stadium of the journey, and the eyes of Artaban, anxiously scanning the great mound of Nimrod and the Temple of the Seven Spheres, could discern no trace of his friends.

. . . At the edge of the terrace he saw a little cairn of broken bricks, and under them a piece of papyrus. He caught it up and read: "We have waited past the midnight, and can delay no longer. We go to find the King. Follow us across the desert."

Artaban sat down upon the ground and covered his head in despair.

"How can I cross the desert," said he, "with no food and with a spent horse? I must return to Babylon, sell my sapphire, and buy a train of camels, and provision for the journey. I may never overtake my friends. Only God the merciful knows whether I shall not lose the sight of the King because I tarried to show mercy."

. . . Artaban [moved] steadily onward, until he arrived at Bethlehem. And it was the third day after the three Wise Men had come to that place and had found Mary and Joseph, with the young child, Jesus, and had laid their gifts of gold and frankincense and myrrh at his feet.

Then the Other Wise Man drew near, weary, but full of hope, bearing his ruby and his pearl to offer to the King. "For now at last," he said, "I shall surely find him, though I be alone, and later than my brethren. This is the place of which the Hebrew exile told me that the prophets had spoken, and here I shall behold the rising of the great light. But I must inquire about the visit of my brethren, and to what house the star directed them, and to whom they presented their tribute."

The streets of the village seemed to be deserted, and Artaban wondered whether the men had all gone up to the hill-pastures to bring down their sheep. From the open door of a cottage he heard the sound of a woman's voice singing softly. He entered and found a young mother hushing her baby to rest. She told him of the strangers from the far East who had appeared in the village three days ago, and how they said that a star had guided them to the place where Joseph of Nazareth was lodging with his wife and her new-born child, and how they had paid reverence to the child and given him many rich gifts.

"But the travellers disappeared again," she continued, "as suddenly as they had come. We were afraid at the strangeness of their visit. We could not understand it. The man of Nazareth took the child and his mother, and fled away that same night secretly, and it was whispered that they were going to Egypt. Ever since, there has been a spell upon the village; something evil hangs over it. They say that the Roman soldiers are coming from Jerusalem to force a new tax from us, and the men have driven the flocks and herds far back among the hills, and hidden themselves to escape it."

Artaban listened to her gentle, timid speech, and the child in her arms looked up in his face and smiled, stretching out its rosy hands to grasp at the winged circle of gold on his breast. His heart warmed to the touch. It seemed like a greeting of love and trust to one who had journeyed long in loneliness and perplexity, fighting with his own doubts and fears, and following a light that was veiled in clouds.

"Why might not this child have been the promised Prince?" he asked within himself, as he touched its soft cheek. "Kings have been born ere now in lowlier houses than this, and the favourite of the stars may rise even from a cottage. But it has not seemed good to the God of wisdom to reward my search so soon and so easily. The one whom I seek has gone before me; and now I must follow the King to Egypt."

The young mother laid the baby in its cradle, and rose to minister to the wants of the strange guest that fate had brought into her house. She set food before him, the plain fare of peasants, but willingly offered, and therefore full of refreshment for the soul as well as for the body. Artaban accepted it gratefully; and, as he ate, the child fell into a happy slumber, and murmured sweetly in its dreams, and a great peace filled the room.

But suddenly there came the noise of a wild confusion in the streets of the village, a shrieking and wailing of women's voices, a clangour of brazen trumpets and a clashing of swords, and a desperate cry: "The soldiers! the soldiers of Herod! They are killing our children."

The young mother's face grew white with terror. She clasped her child to her bosom, and crouched motionless in the darkest corner of the room, covering him with the folds of her robe, lest he should wake and cry.

But Artaban went quickly and stood in the doorway of the house. His broad shoulders filled the portal from side to side, and the peak of his white cap all but touched the lintel.

The soldiers came hurrying down the street with bloody hands and dripping swords. At the sight of the stranger in his imposing dress they hesitated with surprise. The captain of the band approached the threshold to thrust him aside. But Artaban did not stir. His face was as calm as though he were watching the stars, and in his eyes there burned that steady radiance before which even the half-tamed hunting leopard shrinks, and the bloodhound pauses in his leap. He held the soldier silently for an instant, and then said in a low voice:

"I am all alone in this place, and I am waiting to give this jewel to the prudent captain who will leave me in peace."

He showed the ruby, glistening in the hollow of his hand like a great drop of blood.

The captain was amazed at the splendour of the gem. The pupils of his eyes expanded with desire, and the hard lines of greed wrinkled around his lips. He stretched out his hand and took the ruby.

"March on!" he cried to his men, "there is no child here. The house is empty."

The clamor and the clang of arms passed down the street as the headlong fury of the chase sweeps by the secret covert where the trembling deer is hidden. Artaban re-entered the cottage. He turned his face to the east and prayed:

"God of truth, forgive my sin! I have said the thing that is not, to save the life of a child. And two of my gifts are gone. I have spent for man that which was meant for God. Shall I ever be worthy to see the face of the King?"

But the voice of the woman, weeping for joy in the shadow behind him, said very gently:

"Because thou hast saved the life of my little one, may the Lord bless thee and keep thee; the Lord make His face to shine upon thee and be gracious unto thee; the Lord lift up His countenance upon thee and give thee peace."

Three-and-thirty years of the life of Artaban had passed away, and he was still a pilgrim and a seeker after light. . . . Worn and weary and ready to die, but still looking for the King, he had come for the last time to Jerusalem. He had often visited the holy city before, and had searched all its lanes and crowded bevels and black prisons without finding any trace of the family of Nazarenes who had fled from Bethlehem long ago. But now it seemed as if he must make one more effort, and something whispered in his heart that, at last, he might succeed.

It was the season of the Passover. The city was thronged with strangers. The children of Israel, scattered in far lands, had returned to the Temple for the great feast, and there had been a confusion of tongues in the narrow streets for many days.

But on this day a singular agitation was visible in the multitude. . . . Artaban joined a group of people from his own country, Parthian Jews who had come up to keep the Passover, and inquired of them the cause of the tumult, and where they were going.

"We are going," they answered, "to the place called Golgotha, outside the city walls, where there is to be an execution. Have you not heard what has happened? Two famous robbers are to be crucified, and with them another, called Jesus of Nazareth, a man who has done many wonderful works among the people, so that they love him greatly. But the priests and elders have said that he must die, because he gave himself out to be the Son of God. And Pilate has sent him to the cross because he said that he was the 'King of the Jews.'"

How strangely these familiar words fell upon the tired heart of Artaban! They had led him for a lifetime over land and sea. And now they came to him mysteriously, like a message of despair. The King had arisen, but he had been denied and cast out. He was about to perish. Perhaps he was already dying. Could it be the same who had been born in Bethlehem thirty-three years ago, at whose birth the star had appeared in heaven, and of whose coming the prophets had spoken?

Artaban's heart beat unsteadily with that troubled, doubtful apprehension which is the excitement of old age. But he said within himself: "The ways of God are stranger than the thoughts of men, and it may be that I shall find the King, at last, in the hands of his enemies, and shall come in time to offer my pearl for his ransom before he dies."

So the old man followed the multitude with slow and painful steps toward the Damascus gate of the city. Just beyond the entrance of the guardhouse a troop of Macedonian soldiers came down the street, dragging a young girl with torn dress and disheveled hair. As the Magian paused to look at her with compassion, she broke suddenly from the hands of her tormentors, and threw herself at his feet, clasping him around the knees. She had seen his white cap and the winged circle on his breast.

"Have pity on me," she cried, "and save me, for the sake of the God of Purity! I also am a daughter of the true religion which is taught by the

Magi. My father was a merchant of Parthia, but he is dead, and I am seized for his debts to be sold as a slave. Save me from worse than death!"

Artaban trembled.

It was the old conflict in his soul, which had come to him in the palm-grove of Babylon and in the cottage at Bethlehem—the conflict between the expectation of faith and the impulse of love. Twice the gift which he had consecrated to the worship of religion had been drawn to the service of humanity. This was the third trial, the ultimate probation, the final and irrevocable choice. . . .

He took the pearl from his bosom. Never had it seemed so luminous, so radiant, so full of tender, living lustre. He laid it in the hand of the slave.

"This is thy ransom, daughter! It is the last of my treasures which I kept for the King."

While he spoke, the darkness of the sky deepened, and shuddering tremors ran through the earth heaving convulsively like the breast of one who struggles with mighty grief.

The walls of the houses rocked to and fro. Stones were loosened and crashed into the street. Dust clouds filled the air. The soldiers fled in terror, reeling like drunken men. But Artaban and the girl whom he had ransomed crouched helpless beneath the wall of the Praetorium.

What had he to fear? What had he to hope? He had given away the last remnant of his tribute for the King. He had parted with the last hope of finding him. The quest was over, and it had failed. But, even in that thought, accepted and embraced, there was peace. It was not resignation. It was not submission. It was something more profound and searching. He knew that all was well, because he had done the best that he could from day to day. He had been true to the light that had been given to him. He had looked for more. And if he had not found it, if a failure was all that came out of his life, doubtless that was the best that was possible. He had not seen the revelation of "life everlasting, incorruptible and immortal." But he knew that even if he could live his earthly life over again, it could not be otherwise than it had been.

One more lingering pulsation of the earthquake quivered through the ground. A heavy tile, shaken from the roof, fell and struck the old man on the temple. He lay breathless and pale, with his gray head resting on the young girl's shoulder, and the blood trickling from the wound. As she bent over him, fearing that he was dead, there came a voice through the twilight, very small and still, like music sounding from a distance, in which the notes are clear but the words are lost. The girl turned to see if some one had spoken from the window above them, but she saw no one.

Then the old man's lips began to move, as if in answer, and she heard him say in the Parthian tongue:

"Not so, my Lord! For when saw I thee an hungered and fed thee? Or thirsty, and gave thee drink? When saw I thee a stranger, and took thee in? Or naked, and clothed thee? When saw I thee sick or in prison, and came unto thee? Three-and-thirty years have I looked for thee; but I have never seen thy face, nor ministered to thee, my King."

He ceased, and the sweet voice came again. And again the maid heard it, very faint and far away. But now it seemed as though she understood the words:

"Verily I say unto thee, Inasmuch as thou hast done it unto one of the least of these my brethren, thou hast done it unto me."

A calm radiance of wonder and joy lighted the pale face of Artaban like the first ray of dawn, on a snowy mountain-peak. A long breath of relief exhaled gently from his lips.

His journey was ended. His treasures were accepted. The Other Wise Man had found the King. ✧

HENRY VAN DYKE (1852–1933) WAS A PRESBYTERIAN MINISTER, ENGLISH PROFESSOR, AND ACCOMPLISHED ESSAYIST. HE ALSO PENNED THE LYRICS TO "JOYFUL, JOYFUL, WE ADORE THEE," SET TO THE TUNE OF "ODE TO JOY" BY BEETHOVEN.

Never Alone

Henri Nouwen

1983

God came to us because he wanted to join us on the road, to listen to our story, and to help us realize that we are not walking in circles but moving towards the house of peace and joy. This is the great mystery of Christmas that continues to give us comfort and consolation: we are not alone on our journey. The God of love who gave us life sent his only Son to be with us at all times and in all places, so that we never have to feel lost in our struggles but always can trust that he walks with us.

The challenge is to let God be who he wants to be. A part of us clings to our aloneness and does not allow God to touch us where we are most in pain. Often we hide from him precisely those places in ourselves where we feel guilty, ashamed, confused, and lost. Thus we do not give him a chance to be with us where we feel most alone.

Christmas is the renewed invitation not to be afraid and to let him—whose love is greater than our own hearts and minds can comprehend—be our companion.

HENRI NOUWEN (1932–1996), A CATHOLIC PRIEST AND WRITER, WROTE MORE THAN FORTY BOOKS ABOUT SPIRITUALITY. HE ALSO SERVED AS PASTOR FOR A COMMUNITY IN TORONTO THAT CARED FOR PEOPLE WITH DEVELOPMENTAL DISABILITIES. HE IS PERHAPS BEST KNOWN FOR HIS BOOKS THAT EMPHASIZE THE PERSONAL LOVE OF GOD.

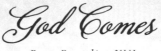

God Comes

Pope Benedict XVI

2006

At the beginning of a new yearly cycle, the liturgy invites the Church to renew her proclamation to all the peoples and sums it up in two words "God comes." These words, so concise, contain an ever new evocative power.

Let us pause a moment to reflect: it is not used in the past tense—God has come, nor in the future—God will come, but in the present—"God comes." At a closer look, this is a continuous present, that is, an ever-continuous action: it happened, it is happening now, and it will happen again. In whichever moment, "God comes." The verb "to come" appears here as a theological verb, indeed theological, since it says something about God's very nature. Proclaiming that "God comes" is equivalent, therefore, to simply announcing God himself, through one of his essential and qualifying features: his being the God-who-comes.

Advent calls believers to become aware of this truth and to act accordingly. It rings out as a salutary appeal in the days, weeks and months that repeat: Awaken! Remember that God comes! Not yesterday, not tomorrow, but today, now!

The one true God, "the God of Abraham, Isaac and Jacob," is not a God who is there in Heaven, unconcerned with us and our history, but he is the-God-who-comes. He is a Father who never stops thinking of us and, in the extreme respect of our freedom, desires to meet us and visit us; he wants to come, to dwell among us, to stay with us. His "coming" is motivated by the desire to free us from evil and death, from all that prevents our true happiness. God comes to save us.

The Fathers of the Church observe that the "coming" of God—continuous and, as it were, co-natural with his very being—is centered in the two principal comings of Christ: his Incarnation and his glorious return at the end of time (cf. Cyril of Jerusalem, Catechesis 15,1: PG 33, 870). The Advent Season lives the whole of this polarity.

In the first days, the accent falls on the expectation of the Lord's Final Coming. With Christmas approaching, the dominant note instead is on the commemoration of the event at Bethlehem, so that we may recognize it as the "fullness of time." Between these two "manifested" comings it is possible to identify a third, which St. Bernard calls "intermediate" and "hidden," and which occurs in the souls of believers and, as it were, builds a "bridge" between the first and the last coming.

POPE BENEDICT XVI, BORN JOSEPH RATZINGER, (1927–) WAS ELECTED TO THE PAPACY IN 2005 AFTER A LONG ACADEMIC CAREER. HE SPEAKS FREQUENTLY ABOUT FRIENDSHIP WITH CHRIST AND ABOUT RESISTING MORAL RELATIVISM.

I do come home at Christmas.
We all do, or we all should. We all come home,
or ought to come home, for a short holiday—the
longer, the better—from the great boarding school
where we are forever working at our arithmetical
slates, to take, and give a rest.

CHARLES DICKENS

In the Bleak Midwinter

Christina Rossetti

1872

In the bleak mid-winter
Frosty wind made moan,
Earth stood hard as iron,
Water like a stone;
Snow had fallen, snow on snow,
Snow on snow,
In the bleak mid-winter
Long ago.

Our God, Heaven cannot hold Him
Nor earth sustain;
Heaven and earth shall flee away
When He comes to reign:
In the bleak mid-winter
A stable-place sufficed
The Lord God Almighty,
Jesus Christ.

Enough for Him, whom cherubim
Worship night and day,
A breastful of milk
And a mangerful of hay;

Enough for Him, whom angels
Fall down before,
The ox and ass and camel
Which adore.

Angels and archangels
May have gathered there,
Cherubim and seraphim
Thronged the air,
But only His mother
In her maiden bliss,
Worshipped the Beloved
With a kiss.

What can I give Him,
Poor as I am?
If I were a shepherd
I would bring a lamb,
If I were a wise man
I would do my part,
Yet what I can I give Him,
Give my heart.

CHRISTINA ROSSETTI (1830–1894) WAS A BRITISH POET WHO WROTE
MANY DEVOTIONAL POEMS, INCLUDING "IN THE BLEAK MIDWINTER"
AND "CHRISTMASTIDE." THIS SELECTION WAS SET TO MUSIC BY GUSTAV
HOLST IN 1906.

My Christmas Miracle

Taylor Caldwell

1961

For many of us, one Christmas stands out from all the others, the one when the meaning of the day shone clearest.

Although I did not guess it, my own truest Christmas began on a rainy spring day in the bleakest year of my life. Recently divorced, I was in my 20's, had no job, and was on my way downtown to go the rounds of the employment offices. I had no umbrella, for my old one had fallen apart, and I could not afford another one. I sat down in the streetcar, and there against the seat was a beautiful silk umbrella with a silver handle inlaid with gold and flecks of bright enamel. I had never seen anything so lovely.

I examined the handle and saw a name engraved among the golden scrolls. The usual procedure would have been to turn in the umbrella to the conductor, but on impulse I decided to take it with me and find the owner myself. I got off the streetcar in a downpour and thankfully opened the umbrella to protect myself. Then I searched a telephone book for the name on the umbrella and found it. I called, and a lady answered.

Yes, she said in surprise, that was her umbrella, which her parents, now dead, had given her for a birthday present. But, she added, it had been stolen from her locker at school (she was a teacher) more than a year before. She was so excited that I forgot I was looking for a job and went directly to her small house. She took the umbrella, and her eyes filled with tears.

The teacher wanted to give me a reward, but—though $20 was all I had in the world—her happiness at retrieving this special possession was such that to have accepted money would have spoiled something. We talked for a while, and I must have given her my address. I don't remember.

The next six months were wretched. I was able to obtain only temporary employment here and there, for a small salary, though this was what they now call the Roaring Twenties. But I put aside 25 or 50 cents when I could afford it for my little girl's Christmas presents. (It took me six months to save $8.) My last job ended the day before Christmas, my $30 rent was soon due, and I had $15 to my name—which Peggy and I would need for food. She was home from her convent boarding school and was excitedly looking forward to her gifts the next day, which I had already purchased. I had bought her a small tree, and we were going to decorate it that night.

The stormy air was full of the sound of Christmas merriment as I walked from the streetcar to my small apartment. Bells rang and children shouted in the bitter dusk of the evening, and windows were lighted and everyone was running and laughing. But there would be no Christmas for me, I knew, no gifts, no remembrance whatsoever. As I struggled through the snowdrifts, I just about reached the lowest point in my life. Unless a miracle happened I would be homeless in January, foodless, jobless. I had prayed steadily for weeks, and there had been no answer but this coldness and darkness, this harsh air, this abandonment. God and men had completely forgotten me. I felt old as death, and as lonely. What was to become of us?

I looked in my mailbox. There were only bills in it, a sheaf of them, and two white envelopes which I was sure contained more bills. I went up three dusty flights of stairs, and I cried, shivering in my thin coat. But I made myself smile so I could greet my little daughter with a pretense of happiness. She opened the door for me and threw herself in my arms, screaming joyously and demanding that we decorate the tree immediately.

Peggy was not yet six years old, and had been alone all day while I worked. She had set our kitchen table for our evening meal, proudly, and put pans out and the three cans of food which would be our dinner. For some reason, when I looked at those pans and cans, I felt broken-hearted. We would have only hamburgers for our Christmas dinner tomorrow, and gelatin. I stood in the cold little kitchen, and misery overwhelmed me. For the first time in my life, I doubted the existence of God and His mercy, and the coldness in my heart was colder than ice.

The doorbell rang, and Peggy ran fleetly to answer it, calling that it must be Santa Claus. Then I heard a man talking heartily to her and went to the door. He was a delivery man, and his arms were full of big parcels, and he was laughing at my child's frenzied joy and her dancing. This is a mistake, I said, but he read the name on the parcels, and they were for me. When he had gone I could only stare at the boxes. Peggy and I sat on the floor and opened them. A huge doll, three times the size of the one I had bought for her. Gloves. Candy. A beautiful leather purse. Incredible! I looked for the name of the sender. It was the teacher, the address simply California, where she had moved.

Our dinner that night was the most delicious I had ever eaten. I could only pray to myself, Thank You, Father. I forgot I had no money for the rent and only $15 in my purse and no job. My child and I ate and laughed together in happiness. Then we decorated the little tree and marveled at it. I put Peggy to bed and set up her gifts around the tree, and a sweet peace flooded me like a benediction. I had some hope again. I could even examine the sheaf of bills without cringing. Then I opened the two white envelopes. One contained a check for $30 from a company I had worked for briefly in the summer. It was, said a note, my Christmas bonus. My rent!

The other envelope was an offer of a permanent position with the government—to begin in two days after Christmas. I sat with the letter in my hand and the check on the table before me, and I think that was the most joyful moment of my life up to that time.

The church bells began to ring. I hurriedly looked at my child, who was sleeping blissfully, and ran down to the street. Everywhere people were walking to church to celebrate the birth of the Savior. People smiled at me and I smiled back. The storm had stopped, the sky was pure and glittering with stars.

"The Lord is born!" sang the bells to the crystal night and the laughing darkness. Someone began to sing, "Come, all ye faithful!" I joined in and sang with the strangers all about me.

I am not alone at all, I thought. I was never alone at all.

And that, of course, is the message of Christmas. We are never alone. Not when the night is darkest, the wind coldest, the world seemingly most indifferent. For this is still the time God chooses.✧

TAYLOR CALDWELL (1900–1985) WAS AN ENGLISH-AMERICAN NOVELIST AND COLUMNIST. HER 1976 NOVEL *The Captains and the Kings* WAS MADE INTO A TV MINISERIES.

Just as those first shepherds heard the celestial music echoing over the countryside, and the Magi from the east discerned that a strange new star had come into their universe, so thousands today are hearing by faith the distant melodies of heaven and are remembering once again the true meaning of Christmas.

BILLY GRAHAM

Reflections on a Tyrant King

Eugene Peterson

2006

While the magi approached the birth of Jesus with reverential awe, Herod, hearing the news, was full of dread. It is possible to fashion values and goals so defiant of God that any rumor of his reality shakes our foundation.

[But] Herod, impressive and fearful to his contemporaries, looks merely ridiculous to us. His secret, lying intrigues are useless before the ingenuous, unarmed invasion of history in Jesus at Bethlehem. [His] threat, which seems so ominous, is scarcely more than a pretext for accomplishing God's will. The flight into Egypt, retracing the ancient route of redemption, is part of a finely wrought salvation history.

The slaughtered children participate in the messianic birth pangs: Christ enters a world flailing in rebellion. Herod, in a tantrum, hysterically tries to hold on to his kingdom. The voice in Ramah reverberates in history's echo chambers and gets louder every year.

Lord, I see that Herod is real enough: he opens scenes, he triggers sequences, but he doesn't cause anything. Evil can't. Only you, God, cause, and what you cause is salvation, through Jesus, my Lord and Savior. Amen.

EUGENE PETERSON (1932–) IS PERHAPS BEST KNOWN FOR HIS BESTSELLING PARAPHRASE OF THE BIBLE, *The Message*. HE HAS WRITTEN MANY OTHER BOOKS ON SPIRITUALITY AND PASTORAL MINISTRY.

The Journey of the Magi

In the time of King Herod, after Jesus was born in Bethlehem of Judea, wise men from the East came to Jerusalem, asking, "Where is the child who has been born king of the Jews? For we observed his star at its rising, and have come to pay him homage." When King Herod heard this, he was frightened, and all Jerusalem with him; and calling together all the chief priests and scribes of the people, he inquired of them where the Messiah was to be born. They told him,

"In Bethlehem of Judea; for so it has been written by the prophet: 'And you, Bethlehem, in the land of Judah, are by no means least among the rulers of Judah; for from you shall come a ruler who is to shepherd my people Israel.'"

Then Herod secretly called for the wise men and learned from them the exact time when the star had appeared. Then he sent them to Bethlehem, saying, "Go and search diligently for the child; and when you have found him, bring me word so that I may also go and pay him homage." When they had heard the king, they set out; and there, ahead of them, went the star that they had seen at its rising, until it stopped over the place where the child was. When they saw that the star had stopped, they were overwhelmed with joy. On entering the house, they saw the child with Mary his mother; and they knelt down and paid him homage. Then, opening their treasure chests, they offered him gifts of gold, frankincense, and myrrh. And having been warned in a dream not to return to Herod, they left for their own country by another road. ✧

—MATTHEW 2:1–12

Giving

The giving of gifts has long been part of
Christmas. Giving a simple, heartfelt gift
to someone in need reminds us of
the giving nature of God.

[Jesus] himself said,
"It is more blessed to give than to receive."

—ACTS 20:35

SANTA CLAUS.

MERRY CHRISTMAS

A Christmas Inspiration

Lucy Maud Montgomery

1901

Well, I really think Santa Claus has been very good to us all,"
said Jean Lawrence, pulling the pins out of her heavy coil
of fair hair and letting it ripple over her shoulders.

"So do I," said Nellie Preston as well as she could with a
mouthful of chocolates. "Those blessed home folks of mine seem to
have divined by instinct the very things I most wanted."

It was the dusk of Christmas Eve and they were all in Jean
Lawrence's room at No. 16 Chestnut Terrace. No. 16 was a
boarding house, and boarding houses are not proverbially cheerful
places in which to spend Christmas, but Jean's room, at least,
was a pleasant spot, and all the girls had brought their Christmas
presents in to show each other. Christmas came on Sunday that
year and the Saturday evening mail at Chestnut Terrace had been
an exciting one.

Jean had lighted the pink-globed lamp on her table and the
mellow light fell over merry faces as the girls chatted about their
gifts. On the table was a big white box heaped with roses that
betokened a bit of Christmas extravagance on somebody's part.

Jean's brother had sent them to her from Montreal, and all the girls were enjoying them in common.

No. 16 Chestnut Terrace was overrun with girls generally. But just now only five were left; all the others had gone home for Christmas, but these five could not go and were bent on making the best of it.

Belle and Olive Reynolds, who were sitting on the bed—Jean could never keep them off it—were High School girls; they were said to be always laughing, and even the fact that they could not go home for Christmas because a young brother had measles did not dampen their spirits.

Beth Hamilton, who was hovering over the roses, and Nellie Preston, who was eating candy, were art students, and their homes were too far away to visit. As for Jean Lawrence, she was an orphan, and had no home of her own. She worked on the staff of one of the big city newspapers and the other girls were a little in awe of her cleverness, but her nature was a "chummy" one and her room was a favorite rendez-vous. Everybody liked frank, open-handed and hearted Jean.

"It was so funny to see the postman when he came this evening," said Olive. "He just bulged with parcels. They were sticking out in every direction."

"We all got our share of them," said Jean with a sigh of content. "Even the cook got six—I counted."

"Miss Allen didn't get a thing—not even a letter," said Beth quickly. Beth had a trick of seeing things that other girls didn't.

"I forgot Miss Allen. No, I don't believe she did," answered Jean thoughtfully as she twisted up her pretty hair. "How dismal it must be to be so forlorn as that on Christmas Eve of all times. Ugh! I'm glad I have friends."

"I saw Miss Allen watching us as we opened our parcels and letters," Beth went on. "I happened to look up once, and such an expression as was on her face, girls! It was pathetic and sad and envious all at once. It really made me feel bad—for five minutes," she concluded honestly.

"Hasn't Miss Allen any friends at all?" asked Beth.

"No, I don't think she has," answered Jean. "She has lived here for fourteen years, so Mrs. Pickrell says. Think of that, girls! Fourteen years at Chestnut Terrace! Is it any wonder that she is thin and dried-up and snappy?"

"Nobody ever comes to see her and she never goes anywhere," said Beth. "Dear me! She must feel lonely now when everybody else is being remembered by their friends. I can't forget her face tonight; it actually haunts me. Girls, how would you feel if you hadn't anyone belonging to you, and if nobody thought about you at Christmas?"

"Ow!" said Olive, as if the mere idea made her shiver.

A little silence followed. To tell the truth, none of them liked Miss Allen. They knew that she did not like them either, but considered them frivolous and pert, and complained when they made a racket.

"The skeleton at the feast," Jean called her, and certainly the presence of the pale, silent, discontented-looking woman at the No. 16 table did not tend to heighten its festivity.

Presently Jean said with a dramatic flourish, "Girls, I have an inspiration—a Christmas inspiration!"

"What is it?" cried four voices.

"Just this. Let us give Miss Allen a Christmas surprise. She has not received a single present and I'm sure she feels lonely. Just think how we would feel if we were in her place."

"That is true," said Olive thoughtfully. "Do you know, girls, this evening I went to her room with a message from Mrs. Pickrell, and I do believe she had been crying. Her room looked dreadfully bare and cheerless, too. I think she is very poor. What are we to do, Jean?"

"Let us each give her something nice. We can put the things just outside of her door so that she will see them whenever she opens it. I'll give her some of Fred's roses too, and I'll write a Christmassy letter in my very best style to go with them," said Jean, warming up to her ideas as she talked.

The other girls caught her spirit and entered into the plan with enthusiasm.

"Splendid!" cried Beth. "Jean, it is an inspiration, sure enough. Haven't we been horribly selfish—thinking of nothing but our own gifts and fun and pleasure? I really feel ashamed."

"Let us do the thing up the very best way we can," said Nellie, forgetting even her beloved chocolates in her eagerness. "The shops are open yet. Let us go up town and invest."

Five minutes later five capped and jacketed figures were scurrying up the street in the frosty, starlit December dusk. Miss Allen in her cold little room heard their gay voices and sighed. She was crying by herself in the dark. It was Christmas for everybody but her, she thought drearily.

In an hour the girls came back with their purchases.

"Now, let's hold a council of war," said Jean jubilantly. "I hadn't the faintest idea what Miss Allen would like so I just guessed wildly. I got her a lace handkerchief and a big bottle of perfume and a painted photograph frame—and I'll stick my own photo in it for fun. That was really all I could afford. Christmas purchases have left my purse dreadfully lean."

"I got her a glove-box and a pin tray," said Belle, "and Olive got her a calendar and Whittier's poems. And besides we are going to give her half of that big plummy fruit cake Mother sent us from home. I'm sure she hasn't tasted anything so delicious for years, for fruit cakes don't grow on Chestnut Terrace and she never goes anywhere else for a meal."

Beth had bought a pretty cup and saucer and said she meant to give one of her pretty watercolors too. Nellie, true to her reputation, had invested in a big box of chocolate creams, a gorgeously striped candy cane, a bag of oranges, and a brilliant lampshade of rose-colored crepe paper to top off with.

"It makes such a lot of show for the money," she explained. "I am bankrupt, like Jean."

"Well, we've got a lot of pretty things," said Jean in a tone of satisfaction. "Now we must do them up nicely. Will you wrap them in tissue paper, girls, and tie them with baby ribbon—here's a box of it—while I write that letter?"

While the others chatted over their parcels Jean wrote her letter, and Jean could write delightful letters. She had a decided talent in that respect, and her correspondents all declared her letters to be things of beauty and joy forever. She put her best into Miss Allen's Christmas letter. Since then she has written many bright and clever things, but I do not believe she ever in her life wrote anything more genuinely original and delightful than that letter. Besides, it breathed the very spirit of Christmas, and all the girls declared that it was splendid.

"You must all sign it now," said Jean, "and I'll put it in one of those big envelopes; and, Nellie, won't you write her name on it in fancy letters?"

Which Nellie proceeded to do, and furthermore embellished the envelope by a border of chubby cherubs, dancing hand in hand around it and a sketch of No. 16 Chestnut Terrace in the corner in lieu of a stamp. Not content with this she hunted out a huge sheet of drawing paper and drew upon it an original pen-and-ink design after her own heart. A dudish cat—Miss Allen was fond of the No. 16 cat if she could be said to be fond of anything—was portrayed seated on a rocker arrayed in smoking jacket and cap with a cigar waved airily aloft in one paw while the other held out a placard bearing the legend "Merry Christmas." A second cat in full street costume bowed politely, hat in paw, and waved a banner inscribed with "Happy New Year," while faintly suggested kittens gambolled around the border. The girls laughed until they cried over it and voted it to be the best thing Nellie had yet done in original work.

All this had taken time and it was past eleven o'clock. Miss Allen had cried herself to sleep long ago and everybody else in Chestnut Terrace was abed when five figures cautiously crept down the hall, headed by Jean with a dim lamp. Outside of Miss Allen's door the procession halted and the girls silently arranged their gifts on the floor.

"That's done," whispered Jean in a tone of satisfaction as they tiptoed back. "And now let us go to bed or Mrs. Pickrell, bless her heart, will be down on us for burning so much midnight oil. Oil has gone up, you know, girls."

It was in the early morning that Miss Allen opened her door. But early as it was, another door down the hall was half open too and five rosy faces were peering cautiously out. The girls had been up for an hour for fear they would miss the sight and were all in Nellie's room, which commanded a view of Miss Allen's door.

That lady's face was a study. Amazement, incredulity, wonder, chased each other over it, succeeded by a glow of pleasure. On the floor before her was a snug little pyramid of parcels topped by Jean's letter. On a chair behind it was a bowl of delicious hot-house roses and Nellie's placard.

Miss Allen looked down the hall but saw nothing, for Jean had slammed the door just in time. Half an hour later when they were going down to breakfast Miss Allen came along the hall with outstretched hands to meet them. She had been crying again, but I think her tears were happy ones; and she was smiling now. A cluster of Jean's roses were pinned on her breast.

"Oh, girls, girls," she said, with a little tremble in her voice, "I can never thank you enough. It was so kind and sweet of you. You don't know how much good you have done me."

Breakfast was an unusually cheerful affair at No. 16 that morning. There was no skeleton at the feast and everybody was beaming. Miss Allen laughed and talked like a girl herself.

"Oh, how surprised I was!" she said. "The roses were like a bit of summer, and those cats of Nellie's were so funny and delightful. And your letter too, Jean! I cried and laughed over it. I shall read it every day for a year."

After breakfast everyone went to Christmas service. The girls went uptown to the church they attended. The city was very beautiful in the morning sunshine. There had been a white frost in the night and the tree-lined avenues and public squares seemed like glimpses of fairyland.

"How lovely the world is," said Jean.

"This is really the very happiest Christmas morning I have ever known," declared Nellie. "I never felt so really Christmassy in my inmost soul before."

"I suppose," said Beth thoughtfully, "that it is because we have discovered for ourselves the old truth that it is more blessed to give than to receive. I've always known it, in a way, but I never realized it before."

"Blessing on Jean's Christmas inspiration," said Nellie. "But, girls, let us try to make it an all-the-year-round inspiration, I say. We can bring a little of our own sunshine into Miss Allen's life as long as we live with her."

"Amen to that!" said Jean heartily. "Oh, listen, girls—the Christmas chimes!"

And over all the beautiful city was wafted the grand old message of peace on earth and good will to all the world.✧

LUCY MAUD MONTGOMERY (1874–1942) FAMOUSLY PENNED THE BELOVED *Anne of Green Gables* SERIES. SHE WROTE PROLIFICALLY— PUBLISHING AROUND FIVE HUNDRED SHORT STORIES AND POEMS AND TWENTY NOVELS—ABOUT LIFE IN HER NATIVE CANADA.

To the American People:
Christmas is not a time or a season
but a state of mind. To cherish peace
and good will, to be plenteous in mercy,
is to have the real spirit of Christmas. If
we think on these things, there will be
born in us a Savior and over us will
shine a star sending its gleam of
hope to the world.

CALVIN COOLIDGE

The Elves

The Brothers Grimm

1812

A shoemaker, by no fault of his own, had become so poor that at last he had nothing left but leather for one pair of shoes. So in the evening, he cut out the shoes which he wished to begin to make the next morning, and as he had a good conscience, he lay down quietly in his bed, commended himself to God, and fell asleep. In the morning, after he had said his prayers, and was just going to sit down to work, the two shoes stood quite finished on his table. He was astounded, and knew not what to say to it. He took the shoes in his hands to observe them closer, and they were so neatly made that there was not one bad stitch in them, just as if they were intended as a masterpiece. Soon after, a buyer came in, and as the shoes pleased him so well, he paid more for them than was customary, and, with the money, the shoemaker was able to purchase leather for two pairs of shoes. He cut them out at night, and next morning was about to set to work with fresh courage; but he had no need to do so, for, when he got up, they were already made, and buyers also were not wanting, who gave him money enough to buy leather for four pairs of shoes. The following morning, too, he found the four pairs made; and so it went on constantly, what he cut out in the evening was finished by the morning, so that he soon had his honest independence again, and at last became a wealthy man.

Now it befell that one evening not long before Christmas, when the man had been cutting out, he said to his wife, before going to bed, "What think you if we were to stay up to-night to see who it is that lends us this helping hand?" The woman liked the idea, and lighted a candle, and then they hid themselves in a corner of the room, behind some clothes which were hanging up there, and watched. When it was midnight, two pretty little naked men came, sat down by the shoemaker's table, took all the work which was cut out before them and began to stitch, and sew, and hammer so skilfully and so quickly with their little fingers that the shoemaker could not turn away his eyes for astonishment. They did not stop until all was done, and stood finished on the table, and they ran quickly away.

Next morning the woman said, "The little men have made us rich, and we really must show that we are grateful for it. They run about so, and have nothing on, and must be cold. I'll tell thee what I'll do: I will make them little shirts, and coats, and vests, and trousers, and knit both of them a pair of stockings, and do thou, too, make them two little pairs of shoes." The man said, "I shall be very glad to do it;" and one night, when everything was ready, they laid their presents all together on the table instead of the cut-out work, and then concealed themselves to see how the little men would behave. At midnight they came bounding in, and wanted to get to work at once, but as they did not find any leather cut out, but only the pretty little articles of clothing, they were at first astonished, and then they showed intense delight. They dressed themselves with the greatest rapidity, putting the pretty clothes on, and singing, "Now we are boys so fine to see, Why should we longer cobblers be?"

Then they danced and skipped and leapt over chairs and benches. At last they danced out of doors. From that time forth they came no more, but as long as the shoemaker lived all went well with him, and all his undertakings prospered.✧

Jakob Ludwig Grimm (1785–1863) and Wilhelm Karl Grimm (1786–1859) published collections of German fairy tales and folktales in the nineteenth century, the first of which was *Kinder- und Hausmärchen*, which contains "The Elves."

Merry Christmas

Louisa May Alcott

1875

In the rush of early morning,
When the red burns through the gray,
And the wintry world lies waiting
For the glory of the day,

Then we hear a fitful rustling
Just without upon the stair,
See two small white phantoms coming,
Catch the gleam of sunny hair.

Are they Christmas fairies stealing
Rows of little socks to fill?
Are they angels floating hither
With their message of good-will?

What sweet spell are these elves weaving,
As like larks they chirp and sing?
Are these palms of peace from heaven
That these lovely spirits bring?

Rosy feet upon the threshold,
Eager faces peeping through,
With the first red ray of sunshine,
Chanting cherubs come in view:

Mistletoe and gleaming holly,
Symbols of a blessed day,
In their chubby hands they carry,
Streaming all along the way.

Well we know them, never weary
Of this innocent surprise;
Waiting, watching, listening always
With full hearts and tender eyes,

While our little household angels,
White and golden in the sun
Greet us with the sweet old welcome,—
"Merry Christmas, every one!"

LOUISA MAY ALCOTT (1832–1888) WAS AN AMERICAN POET AND
NOVELIST BEST KNOWN FOR AUTHORING THE *Little Women* SERIES.
SHE RECEIVED INSTRUCTION FROM SUCH WRITERS AS RALPH WALDO
EMERSON AND NATHANIEL HAWTHORNE.

Susie's Letter from Santa Claus

Mark Twain

1874

My Dear Susie Clemens:
I have received and read all the letters which you and
your little sister have written me by the hand of your mother and
your nurses; I have also read those which you little people have
written me with your own hands—for although you did not use
any characters that are in grown peoples' alphabet, you used the
characters that all children in all lands on earth and in the twinkling
stars use; and as all my subjects in the moon are children and use
no character but that, you will easily understand that I can read
your and your baby sister's jagged and fantastic marks without
any trouble at all. But I had trouble with those letters which you
dictated through your mother and the nurses, for I am a foreigner
and cannot read English writing well. You will find that I made no
mistakes about the things which you and the baby ordered in your
own letters—I went down your chimney at midnight when you
were asleep and delivered them all myself—and kissed both of you,
too, because you are good children, well trained, nice mannered,

and about the most obedient little people I ever saw. But in the letter which you dictated there were some words which I could not make out for certain, and one or two small orders which I could not fill because we ran out of stock. Our last lot of kitchen furniture for dolls has just gone to a very poor little child in the North Star away up, in the cold country above the Big Dipper. Your mama can show you that star and you will say: "Little Snow Flake," (for that is the child's name) "I'm glad you got that furniture, for you need it more than I." That is, you must write that, with your own hand, and Snow Flake will write you an answer. If you only spoke it she wouldn't hear you. Make your letter light and thin, for the distance is great and the postage very heavy.

There was a word or two in your mama's letter which I couldn't be certain of. I took it to be "a trunk full of doll's clothes." Is that it? I will call at your kitchen door about nine o'clock this morning to inquire. But I must not see anybody and I must not speak to anybody but you. When the kitchen doorbell rings, George must be blindfolded and sent to open the door. Then he must go back to the dining room or the china closet and take the cook with him. You must tell George he must walk on tiptoe and not speak—otherwise he will die someday. Then you must go up to the nursery and stand on a chair or the nurse's bed and put your ear to the speaking tube that leads down to the kitchen and when I whistle through it you must speak in the tube and say, "Welcome, Santa Claus!" Then I will ask whether it was a trunk you ordered or not. If you say it was, I shall ask you what color you want the trunk to be. Your mama will help you to name a nice color and then you must tell me every single thing in detail which you want the trunk to contain. Then when I say "Good-by and a merry Christmas to my little Susie Clemens," you must say "Good-by, good old Santa Claus, I thank you very much and please tell that little Snow Flake I will look at her star tonight and she must look down here—I will be right in the west bay window; and every fine night I will look at her star and say, 'I know somebody up there and like her, too.'" Then you must go down into the library and make George close all the doors that open into the main hall, and everybody must keep still for a little while. I will go to the moon and get those things and in a few minutes I will come down the chimney that belongs to the fireplace that is in the hall—if it is a trunk you want—because I couldn't get such a thing as a trunk down the nursery chimney, you know.

People may talk if they want, until they hear my footsteps in the hall. Then you tell them to keep quiet a little while till I go back up the chimney. Maybe you will not hear my footsteps at all—so you may go now and then and peep through the dining-room doors, and by and by you will see that thing which you want, right under the piano in the drawing room—for I shall put it there. If I should leave any snow in the hall, you must tell George to sweep it into the fireplace, for I haven't time to do such things. George must not use a broom, but a rag—else he will die someday. You must watch George and not let him run into danger. If my boot should leave a stain on the marble, George must not holystone it away. Leave it there always in memory of my visit; and whenever you look at it or show it to anybody you must let it remind you to be a good little girl. Whenever you are naughty and somebody points to that mark which your good old Santa Claus's boot made on the marble, what will you say, little sweetheart?

Good-by for a few minutes, till I come down to the world and ring the kitchen doorbell.

Your loving Santa Claus—Whom people sometimes call "The Man in the Moon"✧

MARK TWAIN, BORN SAMUEL LANGHORNE CLEMENS, (1835–1910) BECAME FAMOUS AS A WRITER WITH THE PUBLICATION OF HIS FIRST SHORT STORY, "THE CELEBRATED JUMPING FROG OF CALAVARAS COUNTY." HE WENT ON TO WRITE TWENTY-EIGHT BOOKS, INCLUDING *The Adventures of Tom Sawyer* AND *The Adventures of Huckleberry Finn*, AND MANY OTHER STORIES AND SKETCHES.

A Gift from the Heart

Norman Vincent Peale

New York City, where I live, is impressive at any time, but as Christmas approaches, it's overwhelming. Store windows blaze with light and color, furs and jewels. Golden angels, 40 feet tall, hover over Fifth Avenue. Wealth, power, opulence . . . nothing in the world can match this fabulous display.

Through the gleaming canyons, people hurry to find last-minute gifts. Money seems to be no problem. If there's a problem, it's that the recipients so often have everything they need or want that it's hard to find anything suitable, anything that will really say "I love you."

Last December, as Christ's birthday drew near, a stranger was faced with just that problem. She had come from Switzerland to live in an American home and perfect her English. In return, she was willing to act as secretary, mind the grandchildren, do anything that was asked. She was just a girl in her late teens. Her name was Ursula.

One of the tasks her employers gave Ursula was keeping track of Christmas presents as they arrived. There were many, and all would require acknowledgement. Ursula kept a faithful record, but with a growing sense of concern. She was grateful to her American friends; she wanted to show her gratitude by giving them a Christmas present. But nothing that she could buy with her small allowance could compare with the gifts she was recording daily. Besides, even without these gifts, it seemed to her that her employers already had everything.

At night, from her window, Ursula could see the snowy expanse of Central Park, and beyond it the jagged skyline of the city. Far below, in the restless streets, taxis hooted and traffic lights winked red and green. It was so different from the silent majesty of the Alps that at times she had to blink back tears of the homesickness she was careful never to show. It was in the solitude of her little room, a few days before Christmas, that her secret idea came to Ursula.

It was almost as if a voice spoke clearly, inside her head, "It's true," said the voice, "that many people in this city have much more than you do. But surely there are many who have far less. If you will think about this, you may find a solution to what's troubling you."

Ursula thought long and hard. Finally on her day off, which was Christmas Eve, she went to a great department store. She moved slowly along the crowded aisles, selecting and rejecting things in her mind. At last she bought something, and had it wrapped in gaily colored paper. She went out into the gray twilight and looked helplessly around. Finally, she went up to a doorman, resplendent in blue and gold. "Excuse, please," she said in her hesitant English, "can you tell me where to find a poor street?"

"A poor street, miss?" said the puzzled man.

"Yes, a very poor street. The poorest in the city."

The doorman looked doubtful, "Well, you might try Harlem. Or down in the Village. Or the Lower East Side, maybe."

But these names meant nothing to Ursula. She thanked the doorman and walked along, threading her way through the stream of shoppers until she came to a tall policeman. "Please," she said, "can you direct me to a very poor street in . . . in Harlem?"

The policeman looked at her sharply and shook his head. "Harlem's no place for you, miss." And he blew his whistle and sent the traffic swirling past.

Holding her package carefully, Ursula walked on, head bowed against the sharp wind. If a street looked poorer than the one she was on, she took it. But none seemed like the slums she had heard about. Once she stopped a woman, "Please, where do the very poor people live?" But the woman gave her a stare and hurried on.

Darkness came sifting from the sky. Ursula was cold and discouraged and afraid of becoming lost. She came to an intersection and stood forlornly on the corner. What she was trying to do suddenly seemed foolish, impulsive, absurd. Then, through the traffic's roar, she heard the cheerful tinkle of a bell. On the corner opposite, a Salvation Army man was making his traditional Christmas appeal.

At once Ursula felt better, the Salvation Army was a part of life in Switzerland, too. Surely this man could tell her what she wanted to know. She waited for the light, then crossed over to him. "Can you help me? I'm looking for a baby. I have here a little present for the poorest baby I can find." And she held up the package with the green ribbon and the gaily colored paper.

Dressed in gloves and overcoat a size too big for him, he seemed a very ordinary man. But behind his steel-rimmed glasses his eyes were kind. He looked at Ursula and stopped ringing his bell. "What sort of present?" he asked.

"A little dress. For a small, poor baby. Do you know of one?"

"Oh, yes," he said. "Of more than one, I'm afraid."

"Is it far away? I could take a taxi, maybe?"

The Salvation Army man wrinkled his forehead. Finally he said, "It's almost six o'clock. My relief will show up then. If you want to wait, and if you can afford a dollar taxi ride, I'll take you to a family in my own neighborhood who needs just about everything."

"And they have a small baby?"

"A very small baby."

"Then," said Ursula joyfully, "I wait!"

The substitute bell-ringer came. A cruising taxi slowed. In its welcome warmth, she told her new friend about herself, how she came to be in New York, what she was trying to do. He listened in silence, and the taxi driver listened too. When they reached their destination, the driver said, "Take your time, miss. I'll wait for you."

On the sidewalk, Ursula stared up at the forbidding tenement—dark, decaying, saturated with hopelessness. A gust of wind, iron-cold, stirred the refuse in the street and rattled the reeling trashcans. "They live on the third floor," the Salvation Army man said. "Shall we go up?"

But Ursula shook her head. "They would try to thank me, and this is not from me." She pressed the package into his hand. "Take it up for me, please. Say it's from . . . from someone who has everything."

The taxi bore her swiftly from dark streets to lighted ones, from misery to abundance. She tried to visualize the Salvation Army man climbing the stairs, the knock, the explanation, the package being opened, the dress on the baby. It was hard to do.

Arriving at the apartment house on Fifth Avenue where she lived, she fumbled in her purse. But the driver flicked the flag up, "No charge, miss."

"No charge?" echoed Ursula, bewildered.

"Don't worry," the driver said. "I've been paid." He smiled at her and drove away.

Ursula was up early the next day. She set the table with special care. By the time she had finished, the family was awake, and there was all the excitement and laughter of Christmas morning. Soon the living room was a sea of gay discarded wrappings. Ursula thanked everyone for the presents she received. Finally, when there was a lull, she began to explain hesitantly why there seemed to be none from her. She told about going to the department store. She told about the Salvation Army man. She told about the taxi driver. When she finished, there was a long silence. No one seemed to trust himself to speak. "So you see," said Ursula, "I try to do a kindness in your name. And this is my Christmas present to you . . ."

How do I happen to know all this? I know it because ours was the home where Ursula lived. Ours was the Christmas she shared. We were like many Americans, so richly blessed that to this child from across the sea there seemed to be nothing she could add to the material things we already had. And so she offered something of far greater value: a gift from the heart, an act of kindness carried out in our name.

Strange, isn't it? A shy Swiss girl, alone in a great impersonal city. You would think that nothing she could do would affect anyone. And yet, by trying to give away love, she brought the true spirit of Christmas into our lives, the spirit of selfless giving. That was Ursula's secret—and she shared it with us all. ✧

Norman Vincent Peale (1898–1933) was a pastor and writer whose most famous work was 1952's *The Power of Positive Thinking*. His radio program, "The Art of Living," ran for fifty-four years, and he served as editor of the magazine *Guideposts*.

Saint Nicholas

from The Golden Legend

Jacopo da Varagine

1260

Nicholas, a citizen of Patera, was born of rich and pious parents. His father was named Epiphanes, his mother, Johanna. When, in the flower of their youth, they had brought him into the world, they adopted the celibate life thenceforth. While the infant was being bathed on the first day of his life, he stood straight up in the bath. From then on he took the breast only once on Wednesdays and Fridays. As a youth he avoided the dissolute pleasures of his peers, preferring to spend time in churches; and whatever he could understand of the Holy Scriptures he committed to memory.

After the death of his parents he began to consider how he might make use of his great wealth, not in order to win men's praise but to give glory to God. At the time a certain fellow townsman of his, a man of noble origin but very poor, was thinking of prostituting his three virgin daughters in order to make a living out of this vile transaction. When the saint learned of this, abhorring the crime he wrapped a quantity of gold in a cloth and, under cover of darkness, threw it through the window of the other man's house and withdrew unseen. Rising in the morning the man found the gold, gave thanks to God, and celebrated the wedding of his eldest daughter. Not long thereafter the servant of God did the same thing again. This time the man, finding the gold and bursting into loud praises, determined to be on the watch so as to find out who had come to the relief of his penury. Some little time later Nicholas threw a double sum of gold into the house. The noise awakened the man and he pursued the fleeing figure, calling out, "Stop! Stop! Don't hide from me!" and ran faster and faster until he saw that it was Nicholas. Falling to the ground he wanted to kiss his benefactor's feet, but the saint drew away and exacted a promise that the secret would be kept until after his death.

Some time later the bishop of Myra died, and all the bishops of the region gathered to choose a successor. Among them was one bishop of great authority, upon whose opinion the decision of others would depend. This prelate exhorted the others to fast and pray: and that very night he heard a voice telling him to post himself at the doors of the church in the morning, and to consecrate as bishop the first man he saw coming in, whose name would be Nicholas. In the morning he made this known to his colleagues and went outside the church to wait. Meanwhile Nicholas, miraculously guided by God, went early to the church and was the first to enter. The bishop, coming up to him, asked his name; and he, filled with the simplicity of a dove, bowed his head and answered, "Nicholas, the servant of your holiness." Then all the bishops led him in and installed him on the episcopal throne. But he, amidst his honors, always preserved his former humility and gravity of manner. He passed the night in prayer, mortified his body, and shunned the society of women. He was humble in his attitude toward others, persuasive in speech, forceful in counsel, and strict when reprimands were called for. A chronicle also states that Nicholas took part in the Council of Nicaea.✧

The Golden Legend IS A COMPILATION OF FANCIFUL HAGIOGRAPHIES WRITTEN BY JACOPO DA VARAGINE. WHEN PRINTING WAS INVENTED A COUPLE HUNDRED YEARS AFTER THE LEGEND'S COMPLETION, *The Golden Legend* BECAME A POPULAR SELLER.

Are you willing to believe that
love is the strongest thing in the
world—stronger than hate, stronger
than evil, stronger than death—and that
the blessed life which began in Bethlehem
nineteen hundred years ago is the image
and brightness of the Eternal Love?
Then you can keep Christmas.

HENRY VAN DYKE

Mr. Edwards Meets Santa Claus

Laura Ingalls Wilder

1935

The days were short and cold, the wind whistled sharply, but there was no snow. Cold rains were falling. Day after day the rain fell, pattering on the roof and pouring from the eaves.

Mary and Laura stayed close by the fire, sewing their nine-patch quilt blocks, or cutting paper dolls from scraps of wrapping-paper, and hearing the wet sound of the rain. Every night was so cold that they expected to see snow next morning, but in the morning they saw only sad, wet grass.

The pressed their noses against the squares of glass in the windows that Pa had made, and they were glad they could see out. But they wished they could see snow.

Laura was anxious because Christmas was near, and Santa Claus and his reindeer could not travel without snow. Mary was afraid that, even if it snowed, Santa Claus could not find them, so far away in Indian Territory. When they asked Ma about this, she said she didn't know.

"What day is it?" they asked her, anxiously. "How many more days till Christmas?" And they counted off the days on their fingers till there was only one more day left.

Rain was still falling that morning. There was not one crack in the gray sky. They felt almost sure there would be no Christmas. Still, they kept hoping.

Just before noon the light changed. The clouds broke and drifted apart, shining white in a clear blue sky. The sun shone, birds sang, and thousands of drops of water sparkled on the grasses. But when Ma opened the door to let in the fresh, cold air, they heard the creek roaring.

They had not thought about the creek. Now they knew they would have no Christmas, because Santa could not cross that roaring creek.

Pa came in, bringing a big fat turkey. If it weighed less than twenty pounds, he said, he'd eat it, feathers and all. He asked Laura, "How's that for a Christmas dinner? Think you can manage one of those drumsticks?"

She said, yes, she could. But she was sober. Then Mary asked him if the creek was going down, and he said it was still rising.

Ma said it was too bad. She hated to think of Mr. Edwards eating his bachelor cooking all alone on Christmas day. Mr. Edwards had been asked to eat Christmas dinner with them, but Pa shook his head and said a man would risk his neck, trying to cross that creek now.

"No," he said. "That current's too strong. We'll just have to make up our minds that Edwards won't be here tomorrow."

Of course of that meant that Santa Claus could not come, either.

Laura and Mary tried not to mind too much. They watched Ma dress the wild turkey, and it was a very fat turkey. They were lucky little girls, to have a good house to live in, and a warm fire to sit by, and such a turkey for their Christmas dinner. Ma said so, and it was true. Ma said it was too bad that Santa Claus couldn't come this year, but they were such good girls that he hadn't forgotten them; he would surely come next year.

Still, they were not happy.

After supper that night they washed their hands and faces, buttoned their red-flannel nightgowns, tied their night-cap strings, and soberly said their prayers. They lay down in bed and pulled the covers up. It did not seem at all like Christmas.

Pa and Ma sat silent by the fire. After a while Ma asked why Pa didn't play the fiddle and he said, "I don't seem to have the heart to, Caroline."

After a longer while, Ma suddenly stood up.

"I'm going to hang up your stockings, girls," she said. "Maybe something will happen."

Laura's heart jumped. But then she thought again of the creek and she knew nothing could happen.

Ma took one of Mary's clean stockings and one of Laura's, and she hung them from the mantel-shelf, on either side of the fireplace. Laura and Mary watched her over the edge of their bed-covers.

"Now go to sleep," Ma said, kissing them good night. "Morning will come quicker if you're asleep."

She sat down again by the fire and Laura almost went to sleep.

Then she heard Jack growl savagely. The door-latch rattled and someone said, "Ingalls! Ingalls!" Pa was stirring up the fire, and when he opened the door Laura saw that it was morning. The outdoors was gray.

"Great fishhooks, Edwards! Come in, man! What's happened?" Pa exclaimed.

Laura saw the stockings limply dangling, and she scrooged her shut eyes into the pillow.

She heard Pa piling wood on the fire, and she heard Mr. Edwards say he had carried his clothes on his head when he swam the creek. His teeth rattled and his voice shivered. He would be all right, he said, as soon as he got warm.

"It was too big a risk, Edwards," Pa said. "We're glad you're here, but that was too big a risk for a Christmas dinner."

"Your little ones had to have a Christmas," Mr. Edwards replied. "No creek could stop me, after I fetched them their gifts from Independence."

Laura sat straight up in bed. "Did you see Santa Claus?" she shouted.

"I sure did," Mr. Edwards said.

"Where? When? What did he look like? What did he say? Did he really give you something for us?" Mary and Laura cried.

"Wait, wait a minute!" Mr. Edwards laughed. And Ma said she would put the presents in the stockings as Santa Claus intended. She said they mustn't look.

Mr. Edwards came sat on the floor by their bed, and he answered every question they asked him. They honestly tried not to look at Ma, and they didn't quite see what she was doing.

When he saw the creek rising, Mr. Edwards said, he had known that Santa Claus could not get across it. ("But you crossed it," Laura said. "Yes," Mr. Edwards replied, "but Santa Claus is too old and fat. He couldn't make it, where a long, lean razor-back like me could do so.") And Mr. Edwards reasoned that if Santa Claus couldn't cross the creek, likely he would come no farther south than Independence. Why should he come forty miles across the prairie, only to be turned back? Of course he wouldn't do that!

So Mr. Edwards had walked to Independence. ("In the rain?" Mary asked. Mr. Edwards said he wore his rubber coat.) And there, coming down the street in Independence, he had met Santa Claus. ("In the daytime?" Laura asked. She hadn't thought that anyone could see Santa Claus in the daytime. No, Mr. Edwards said; it was night, but light shone out across the street from the saloons.)

Well, the first thing Santa Claus said was, "Hello, Edwards!" ("Did he know you?" Mary asked, and Laura asked, "How did you know he was really Santa Claus?" Mr. Edwards said that Santa Claus knew everybody. And he had recognized Santa at once by his whiskers. Santa Claus had the longest, thickest, whitest set of whiskers west of Mississippi.)

So Santa Claus said, "Hello, Edwards! Last time I saw you, you were sleeping on a corn-shuck bed in Tennessee." And Mr. Edwards well remembered the little pair of red-yarn mittens that Santa Claus had left for him that time.

Then Santa Claus said, "I understand you're living now down along the Verdigris River. Have you ever met up, down yonder, with two little young girls named Mary and Laura?"

"I surely am acquainted with them," Mr. Edwards replied.

"It rests heavy on my mind," said Santa Claus. "They are both of them sweet, pretty, good little young things, and I know they are expecting me. I surely do hate to disappoint two good little girls like them, yet with the water up the way it is, I can't ever make it across that creek. I can figure no way whatsoever to get to their cabin this year, Edwards," Santa Claus said. "Would you do me the favor to fetch them their gifts this one time?"

"I'll do that, and with pleasure," Mr. Edwards told him.

Then Santa Claus and Mr. Edwards stepped across the street to the hitching-posts where the pack-mule was tied. ("Didn't he have his reindeer?" Laura asked. "You know he couldn't," Mary said, "There isn't any snow." "Exactly," said Mr. Edwards. Santa Claus traveled with a pack-mule in the southwest.)

And Santa Claus uncinched the pack and looked through it, and he took out the presents for Mary and Laura.

"Oh, what are they?" Laura cried; but Mary asked, "Then what did he do?"

Then he shook hands with Mr. Edwards, and he swung up on his fine bay horse. Santa Claus rode well, for a man of his weight and build. And he tucked his long, white whiskers under his bandana. "So long, Edwards," he said, and he rode away on the Fort Dodge trail, leading his pack-mule and whistling. Laura and Mary were silent an instant, thinking of that. Then Ma said, "You may now look, girls."

Something was shining bright in the top of Laura's stocking. She squealed and jumped out of bed. So did Mary, but Laura beat her to the fireplace. And the shining thing was a glittering new tin cup. Mary had one exactly like it.

These new tin cups were their very own. Now they each had a cup to drink out of. Laura jumped up and down and shouted and laughed, but Mary stood still and looked with shining eyes at her own tin cup.

Then they plunged their hands into the stockings again. And they pulled out two long, long sticks of candy. It was peppermint candy, striped red and white. They looked and looked at that beautiful candy, and Laura licked her stick, just one lick. But Mary was not so greedy. She didn't take even one lick of her stick.

Those stockings weren't empty yet. Mary and Laura pulled out two small packages. They unwrapped them, and each found a little heart-shaped cake. Over their delicate brown tops was sprinkled white sugar. The sparkling grains lay like tiny drifts of snow.

The cakes were too pretty to eat. Mary and Laura just looked at them. But at last Laura turned hers over, and she nibbled a tiny nibble from underneath, where it wouldn't show. And the inside of that little cake was white!

It had been made of pure white flour, and sweetened with white sugar.

Laura and Mary never would have looked in their stockings again. The cups and the cakes and the candy were almost too much. They were too happy to speak. But Ma asked if they were sure the stockings were empty.

Then they put their arms down inside them, to make sure.

And in the very toe of each stocking was a shining, bright, new penny!

They had never even thought of such a thing as having a penny. Think of having a whole penny for your very own. Think of having a cup and a cake and a stick of candy and a penny.

There never had been such a Christmas.

Now of course, right away, Laura and Mary should have thanked Mr. Edwards for bringing those lovely presents all the way from Independence. But they had forgotten all about Mr. Edwards.

They had even forgotten Santa Claus. In a minute they would have remembered, but before they did, Ma said, gently, "Aren't you going to thank Mr. Edwards?"

"Oh, thank you, Mr. Edwards! Thank you!" they said, and they meant it with all their hearts. Pa shook Mr. Edwards' hand, too, and shook it again. Pa and Ma and Mr. Edwards acted as if they were almost crying. Laura didn't know why. So she gazed again at her beautiful presents.

She looked up again when Ma gasped. And Mr. Edwards was taking sweet potatoes out of his pockets. He said they had helped to balance the package on his head when he swam across the creek. He thought Pa and Ma might like them, with the Christmas turkey.

There were nine sweet potatoes. Mr. Edwards had brought them all the way from town, too. It was just too much. Pa said so. "It's too much, Edwards," he said. They never could thank him enough.

Mary and Laura were much too excited to eat breakfast. They drank the milk from their shining new cups, but they could not swallow the rabbit stew and the cornmeal mush.

"Don't make them, Charles," Ma said. "It will soon be dinnertime."

For Christmas dinner there was the tender, juicy, roasted turkey. There were the sweet potatoes, baked in the ashes and carefully wiped so that you could eat the good skins, too. There was a loaf of salt-rising bread made from the last of the white flour.

And after all that there were stewed dried blackberries and little cakes. But these little cakes were made with brown sugar and they did not have white sugar sprinkled over the tops.

Then Pa and Ma and Mr. Edwards sat by the fire and talked about Christmas times back in Tennessee and up north in the Big Woods. But Mary and Laura looked at their beautiful cakes and played with their pennies and drank water out of their new cups. And little by little they licked and sucked their sticks of candy, till each stick was sharp-pointed on one end.

It was a happy Christmas.✧

Baboushka

A Russian Folk Tale

Date Unknown

It was the night that Jesus was born in Bethlehem. In a faraway country an old woman named Baboushka sat in her snug little house by her warm fire. The wind was drifting the snow outside and howling down the chimney, but it only made Baboushka's fire burn more brightly.

"How glad I am to be indoors," said Baboushka, holding out her hands to the bright blaze.

Suddenly she heard a loud rap at her door. She opened it and there stood three splendidly dressed old men. Their beards were as white as the snow and so long they almost reached the ground. Their eyes shone kindly in the light of Baboushka's candle, and their arms were full of precious things—boxes of jewels and sweet-smelling oils and ointments.

"We have traveled far, Baboushka," they said, "and we have stopped to tell you of the babe born this night in Bethlehem. He has come to rule the world and teach us to be more loving and true. We are bringing Him gifts. Come with us, Baboushka."

Baboushka looked at the swirling, drifting snow and then inside at her cozy room and the crackling fire. "It is too late for me to go with you, good sirs," she said. "The night is too cold." She shut the door and went inside and the old men journeyed to Bethlehem without her.

But as Baboushka sat rocking by her fire, she began to think about the baby Prince, for she loved babies.

"Tomorrow I will go to find Him," she said, "tomorrow, when it is light, and I will carry Him some toys."

In the morning Baboushka put on her long cloak and took her staff, and she filled her basket with the pretty things a baby would like, gold balls, and wooden toys and strings of silver cobwebs, and she set out to find the baby.

But Baboushka had forgotten to ask the three old men the way to Bethlehem, and they had traveled so far during the night that she could not catch up with them. Up and down the road she hurried, through the woods and fields and towns, telling everyone she met, "I am looking for the baby Prince. Where does He lie? I have some pretty toys for Him."

But no one could tell her the way. "Farther on, Baboushka, farther on," was their only reply. So she traveled on and on for years and years—but she never found the little Prince.

They say that Baboushka is traveling still, looking for Him. And every year, when Christmas Eve comes and all the children are lying fast asleep, Baboushka trudges softly through the snowy fields and towns, wrapped in her long cloak and carrying her basket on her arm. Gently she raps at every door.

"Is He here?" she asks. "Is the baby Prince here?" But the answer is always no, and sorrowfully she starts on her way again. Before she leaves, though, she lays a toy from her basket beside the pillow of each child. "For His sake," she says softly, and then hurries on through the years, forever in search of the baby Prince.✧

THIS STORY REPLACES THE SAINT NICHOLAS LEGEND IN RUSSIA AND HAS BEEN TOLD FOR MANY YEARS.

Christmas Every Day

William Dean Howells

1892

The little girl came into her papa's study, as she always did Saturday morning before breakfast, and asked for a story. He tried to beg off that morning, for he was very busy, but she would not let him. So he began:

"Well, once there was a little pig—"

She stopped him at the word. She said she had heard little pig-stories till she was perfectly sick of them.

"Well, what kind of story *shall* I tell, then?"

"About Christmas. It's getting to be the season."

"Well!" Her papa roused himself. "Then I'll tell you about the little girl that wanted it Christmas every day in the year. How would you like that?"

"First-rate!" said the little girl; and she nestled into comfortable shape in his lap, ready for listening.

"Very well, then, this little pig—Oh, what are you pounding me for?"

"Because you said little pig instead of little girl."

"I should like to know what's the difference between a little pig and a little girl that wanted it Christmas every day!"

"Papa!" said the little girl warningly. At this her papa began to tell the story.

Once there was a little girl who liked Christmas so much that she wanted it to be Christmas every day in the year, and as soon as Thanksgiving was over she began to send postcards to the old Christmas Fairy to ask if she mightn't have it. But the old Fairy never answered, and after a while the little girl found out that the Fairy wouldn't notice anything but real letters sealed outside with a monogram—or your initial, anyway. So, then, she began to send letters, and just the day before Christmas, she got a letter from the Fairy, saying she might have it Christmas every day for a year, and then they would see about having it longer.

The little girl was excited already, preparing for the old-fashioned, once-a-year Christmas that was coming the next day. So she resolved to keep the Fairy's promise to herself and surprise everybody with it as it kept coming true, but then it slipped out of her mind altogether.

She had a splendid Christmas. She went to bed early, so as to let Santa Claus fill the stockings, and in the morning she was up the first of anybody and found hers all lumpy with packages of candy, and oranges and grapes, and rubber balls, and all kinds of small presents. Then she waited until the rest of the family was up, and she burst into the library to look at the large presents laid out on the library table—books, and boxes of stationery, and dolls, and little stoves, and dozens of handkerchiefs, and inkstands, and skates, and photograph frames, and boxes of watercolors, and dolls' houses— and the big Christmas tree, lighted and standing in the middle.

She had a splendid Christmas all day. She ate so much candy that she did not want any breakfast, and the whole forenoon the presents kept pouring in that had not been delivered the night before, and she went round giving the presents she had got for other people, and came home and ate turkey and cranberry for dinner, and plum pudding and nuts and raisins and oranges, and then went out and coasted, and came in with a stomachache crying, and her papa said he would see if his house was turned into that sort of fool's paradise another year, and they had a light supper, and pretty early everybody went to bed cross.

Here the little girl pounded her papa in the back, again.

"Well, what now? Did I say pigs?"

"You made them act like pigs."

"Well, didn't they?"

"No matter; you oughtn't put it into a story."

"Very well, then, I'll take it all out."

Her father went on:

The little girl slept very heavily and very late, but she was wakened at last by the other children dancing around her bed with their stockings full of presents in their hands.

"Christmas! Christmas! Christmas!" they all shouted.

"Nonsense! It was Christmas yesterday," said the little girl, rubbing her eyes sleepily.

Her brothers and sisters just laughed. "We don't know about that. It's Christmas today, anyway. You come into the library and see."

Then all at once it flashed on the little girl that the Fairy was keeping her promise, and her year of Christmases was beginning. She was dreadfully sleepy, but she sprang up like a lark—a lark that had overeaten itself and gone to bed cross—and darted into the library. There it was again. Books, and portfolios, and boxes of stationery, and breastpins—

"You needn't go over it all, papa; I guess I can remember just what was there," said the little girl.

Well, and there was the Christmas-tree blazing away, and the family picking out their presents, but looking pretty sleepy, and her father perfectly puzzled, and her mother ready to cry. "I'm sure I don't see how I'm to dispose of all these things," said her mother, and her father said it seemed to him they had had something just like it the day before, but he supposed he must have dreamed it. This struck the little girl as the best kind of a joke; and so she ate so much candy she didn't want any breakfast, and went round carrying presents, and had turkey and cranberry for dinner, and then went out and coasted, and came in with a—

"Papa!"

"Well, what now?"

"What did you promise, you forgetful thing?"

"Oh! oh yes!"

Well, the next day, it was just the same thing over again, but everybody getting crosser; and at the end of a week's time so many people had lost their tempers that you could pick up lost tempers anywhere; they perfectly strewed the ground. Even when people tried to recover their tempers they usually got somebody else's, and it made the most dreadful mix.

The little girl began to get frightened, keeping the secret all to herself; she wanted to tell her mother, but she didn't dare to; and she was ashamed to ask the Fairy to take back her gift, it seemed ungrateful and ill-bred, and she thought she would try to stand it, but she hardly knew how she could, for a whole year. So it went on and on, and it was Christmas on St. Valentine's Day and Washington's Birthday, just the same as any day, and it didn't skip even the First of April, though everything was counterfeit that day, and that was some *little* relief.

After a while coal and potatoes began to be awfully scarce, so many had been wrapped up in tissue-paper to fool papas and mammas with. Turkeys got to be about a thousand dollars apiece—

"Papa!"

"Well, what?"

"You're beginning to fib."

"Well, *two* thousand, then."

And they got to passing off almost anything for turkeys—half-grown humming-birds, and even rocs out of the *Arabian Nights*—the real turkeys were so scarce. And cranberries—well, they asked a diamond apiece for cranberries. All the woods and orchards were cut down for Christmas-trees, and where the woods and orchards used to be it looked just like a stubble-field, with the stumps. After a while they had to make Christmas-trees out of rags, and stuff them with bran, like old-fashioned dolls; but there were plenty of rags, because people got so poor, buying presents for one another, that they couldn't get any new clothes, and they just wore their old ones to tatters. They got so poor that everybody had to go to the poor-house, except the confectioners, and the fancy-store keepers, and the picture-book sellers, and the expressmen; and *they* all got so rich and proud that they would hardly wait upon a person when he came to buy. It was perfectly shameful!

Well, after it had gone on about three or four months, the little girl, whenever she came into the room in the morning and saw those great ugly, lumpy stockings dangling at the fire-place, and the disgusting presents around everywhere, used to just sit down and burst out crying. In six months she was perfectly exhausted; she couldn't even cry any more; she just lay on the lounge and rolled her eyes and panted. About the beginning of October she took to sitting down on dolls wherever she found them—French dolls, or any kind—she hated the sight of them so; and by

Thanksgiving she was crazy, and just slammed her presents across the room.

By that time people didn't carry presents around nicely any more. They flung them over the fence, or through the window, or anything; and, instead of running their tongues out and taking great pains to write "For dear Papa," or "Mamma," or "Brother," or "Sister," or "Susie," or "Sammie," or "Billie," or "Bobbie," or "Jimmie," or "Jennie," or whoever it was, and troubling to get the spelling right, and then signing their names, and "Xmas, 18—," they used to write in the gift-books, "Take it, you horrid old thing!" and then go and bang it against the front door. Nearly everybody had built barns to hold their presents, but pretty soon the barns overflowed, and then they used to let them lie out in the rain, or anywhere. Sometimes the police used to come and tell them to shovel their presents off the sidewalk, or they would arrest them.

"I thought you said everybody had gone to the poor-house," interrupted the little girl.

"They did go, at first," said her papa; "but after a while the poor-houses got so full that they had to send the people back to their own houses. They tried to cry, when they got back, but they couldn't make the least sound."

"Why couldn't they?"

"Because they had lost their voices, saying 'Merry Christmas' so much. Did I tell you how it was on the Fourth of July?"

"No; how was it?"

And the little girl nestled closer, in expectation of something uncommon.

Well, the night before, the boys stayed up to celebrate, as they always do, and fell asleep before twelve o'clock, as usual, expecting to be wakened by the bells and cannon. But it was nearly eight o'clock before the first boy in the United States woke up, and then he found out what the trouble was. As soon as he could get his clothes on he ran out of the house and smashed a big cannon-torpedo down on the pavement; but it didn't make any more noise than a damp wad of paper; and after he tried about twenty or thirty more, he began to pick them up and look at them. Every single torpedo was a big raisin!

Then he just streaked it up-stairs, and examined his fire-crackers and toy-pistol and two-dollar collection of fireworks, and found that they were nothing but sugar and candy painted up to look like fireworks! Before ten o'clock every boy in the United States found out that his Fourth of July things had turned into Christmas things; and then they just sat down and cried—they were so mad. There are about twenty million boys in the United States, and so you can imagine what a noise they made. Some men got together before night, with a little powder that hadn't turned into purple sugar yet, and they said they would fire off *one* cannon, anyway. But the cannon burst into a thousand pieces, for it was nothing but rock-candy, and some of the men nearly got killed. The Fourth of

July orations all turned into Christmas carols, and when anybody tried to read the Declaration, instead of saying, "When in the course of human events it becomes necessary," he was sure to sing, "God rest you, merry gentlemen." It was perfectly awful.

The little girl drew a deep sigh of satisfaction.

"And how was it at Thanksgiving?"

Her papa hesitated. "Well, I'm almost afraid to tell you. I'm afraid you'll think it's wicked."

"Well, tell, anyway," said the little girl.

Well, before it came Thanksgiving it had leaked out who had caused all these Christmases. The little girl had suffered so much that she had talked about it in her sleep; and after that hardly anybody would play with her. People just perfectly despised her, because if it had not been for her greediness it wouldn't have happened; and now, when it came Thanksgiving, and she wanted them to go to church, and have squash-pie and turkey, and show their gratitude, they said that all the turkeys had been eaten up for her old Christmas dinners, and if she would stop the Christmases, they would see about the gratitude. Wasn't it dreadful? And the very next day the little girl began to send letters to the Christmas Fairy, and then telegrams, to stop it. But it didn't do any good; and then she got to calling at the Fairy's house, but the girl that came to the door always said, "Not at home," or "Engaged," or "At dinner," or something like that; and so it went on till it came to the old once-a-year Christmas Eve. The little girl fell asleep, and when she woke up in the morning—

"She found it was all nothing but a dream," suggested the little girl.

"No, indeed!" said her papa. "It was all every bit true!"

"Well, what *did* she find out, then?"

"Why, that it wasn't Christmas at last, and wasn't ever going to be, any more. Now it's time for breakfast."

The little girl held her papa fast around the neck.

"You sha'n't go if you're going to leave it *so*!"

"How do you want it left?"

"Christmas once a year."

"All right," said her papa; and he went on again.

Well, there was the greatest rejoicing all over the country, and it extended clear up into Canada. The people met together everywhere, and kissed and cried for joy. The city carts went around and gathered up all the candy and raisins and nuts, and dumped them into the river; and it made the fish perfectly sick; and the whole United States, as far out as Alaska, was one blaze of bonfires, where the children were burning up their gift-books and presents of all kinds. They had the greatest *time*!

The little girl went to thank the old Fairy because she had stopped its being Christmas, and she said she hoped she would keep her promise and see that Christmas never, never came again. Then the Fairy frowned, and asked her if she was sure she knew what she meant; and the little girl asked her, Why not? and the old Fairy said that now she was behaving just as greedily as ever, and she'd better look out. This made the little girl think it all over carefully again, and she said she would be willing to have it Christmas about once in a thousand years; and then she said a hundred, and then she said ten, and at last she got down to one. Then the Fairy said that was the good old way that had pleased people ever since Christmas began, and she was agreed. Then the little girl said, "What're your shoes made of?" And the Fairy said, "Leather." And the little girl said, "Bargain's done forever," and skipped off, and hippity-hopped the whole way home, she was so glad.

"How will that do?" asked the papa.

"First-rate!" said the little girl; but she hated to have the story stop, and was rather sober.

However, her mamma put her head in at the door, and asked her papa:

"Are you never coming to breakfast? What have you been telling that child?"

"Oh, just a moral tale."

The little girl caught him around the neck again.

"*We* know! Don't you tell *what*, papa! Don't you tell *what*!"✧

WILLIAM DEAN HOWELLS (1837–1920) WROTE OVER ONE HUNDRED BOOKS IN A BROAD RANGE OF GENRES, INCLUDING A CAMPAIGN BIOGRAPHY FOR ABRAHAM LINCOLN. HE SERVED AS THE FIRST PRESIDENT OF THE AMERICAN ACADEMY OF ARTS AND LETTERS.

Joy

At Christmastime, heaven and nature
truly seem to sing—joyful choirs, cheerful
decorations, and chiming bells—as well as the
deep-down joy of celebrating the Savior's birth.

*Do not be afraid; for see—I am bringing
you good news of great joy for all the people:
to you is born this day in the city of David
a Savior, who is the Messiah, the LORD.*

—LUKE 2:10–11

Christmas and the Professors

G. K. Chesterton

1909

There is one very vile habit that the pedants have, and that is explaining to a man why he does a thing which the man himself can explain quite well—and quite differently. If I go down on all-fours to find sixpence, it annoys me to be told by a passing biologist that I am really doing it because my remote ancestors were quadrupeds. I concede that he knows all about biology, or even a great deal about my ancestors; but I know he is wrong, because he does not know about the sixpence. If I climb a tree after a stray cat, I am unconvinced when a stray anthropologist tells me that I am doing it because I am essentially arboreal and barbaric. I happen to know why I am doing it; and I know it is because I am amiable and somewhat over-civilized. Scientists will talk to a man on general guesswork about things that they know no more about than about his pocket money or his pet cat. Religion is one of them, and all the festivals and formalities that are rooted in religion. Thus a man will tell me that in keeping Christmas I am not keeping a Christian feast, but a pagan feast. This is exactly as if he told me that I was not feeling furiously angry, but only a little sad. I know how I am feeling all right; and why I am feeling it. I know this in the case of cats, sixpences, anger, and Christmas Day. When a learned man tells me that on the 25th of December I am really astronomically worshipping the sun, I answer that I am not. I am practicing a particular personal religion, the pleasures of which (right or wrong) are not in the least astronomical. If he says that the cult of Christmas and the cult of Apollo are the same, I answer that they are utterly different; and I ought to know, for I have held both of them. I believed in Apollo when I was quite little; and I believe in Christmas now that I am very, very big.

Let us not take with such smooth surrender these tenth-truths at tenth hand, such as the phrase that Christmas is pagan in origin. Let us note exactly how much it really means. It amounts, so far as our knowledge goes, solely to this—that primitive Scandinavians did hold a feast in midwinter. What the dickens else could primitive Scandinavians do, especially in winter? That they put on the largest log in winter: do the professors expect such simple pagans to put on the largest log in summer? It amounts to this, again—that many tribes have either worshipped the sun or (more probably) compared some god or hero to the sun. Just so many a poet has compared his lady to the sun—without by any means intending that she was a Solar Myth. Thus, by talking a great deal about the solar solstice, it can be maintained that Christmas is a sort of sun-worship; to all of which the simple answer is that it feels quite different. If people profess to feel 'the spirit' behind symbols, the first thing I expect of them is that they shall feel how opposite are the adoration of the sun and the following of the star.✧

G. K. Chesterton (1874–1936), a prolific English author, was known as a sharp social and literary critic, a Christian apologist, mystery writer, playwright, and even a poet. C. S. Lewis credits Chesterton's *The Everlasting Man* with his own spiritual conversion.

Mary's Song of Praise

And Mary said,

"My soul magnifies the LORD,

And my spirit rejoices in God my Savior,

for he has looked with favor on the lowliness of his servant.

Surely, from now on all generations will call me blessed;

for the Mighty One has done great things for me,

and holy is his name.

His mercy is for those who fear him

from generation to generation.

He has shown strength with his arm;

he has scattered the proud in the thoughts of their hearts.

He has brought down the powerful from their thrones

and lifted up the lowly;

he has filled the hungry with good things,

and sent the rich away empty.

He has helped his servant Israel

in remembrance of his mercy,

according to the promise he made to our ancestors,

to Abraham and to his descendants forever."

—LUKE 1:46–55

Joy to the World

Isaac Watts

1719

Joy to the world! The Lord is come.
Let Earth receive her King.
Let ev'ry heart prepare Him room,
And Heav'n and Nature sing,
And Heav'n and Nature sing,
And Heav'n, and Heav'n and Nature sing.

Joy to the world! The Savior reigns.
Let men their songs employ,
While fields and floods, rocks, hills, and plains
Repeat the sounding joy,
Repeat the sounding joy,
Repeat, repeat the sounding joy.

He rules the world with truth and grace
And makes the nations prove
The glories of His righteousness
And wonders of His love,
And wonders of His love,
And wonders, wonders of His love.

Christmas in the Olden Time

Sir Walter Scott

1886

Heap on more wood!—the wind is chill;
But let it whistle as it will,
We'll keep our Christmas merry still.
Each age has deemed the new born year
The fittest time for festal cheer.
And well our Christian sires of old.
Loved when the year its course had rolled,
And brought blithe Christmas back again,
With all his hospitable train.
Domestic and religious rite
Gave honour to the holy night:
On Christmas eve the bells were rung;
On Christmas eve the mass was sung;
That only night, in all the year,
Saw the stoled priest the chalice rear.
The damsel donned her kirtle sheen;
The hail was dressed with holly green;
Forth to the wood did merry men go,
To gather in the mistletoe,
Then opened wide the baron's hail
To vassal, tenant, serf, and all;
Power laid his rod of rule aside,

And ceremony doff'd his pride.
The heir, with roses in his shoes,
That night might village partner choose.
The lord, underogating, share
The vulgar game of "post and pair!"
All hailed with uncontroll'd delight
And general voice, the happy night
That to the cottage, as the crown,
Brought tidings of salvation down.
The fire with well dried logs supplied,
Went roaring up the chimney wide;
The huge hail table's oaken face,
Scrubb'd till it shone, the day to grace,
Bore then upon: its massive board
No mark to part the squire and lord.
Then was brought in the lusty brawn,
By old, blue-coated serving-man;
Then the grim boar's head frowned on high,
Crested with bays and rosemary.
Well can the green-garbed ranger tell,
How, when, and where, the monster fell;
What dogs before his death he tore,
And all the baiting of the boar.
The wassail round in good brown bowls,
Garnished with ribbon, blithely trowls.
There the huge sirloin reeked: hard by
Plum-porridge stood, and Christmas pie;

Nor failed old Scotland to produce
At such high tide her savoury goose.
Then came the merry masquers in,
And carols roar'd with blithesome din;
If unmelodious was the song,
It was a hearty note, and strong.
Who lists may in their mumming see
Traces of ancient mystery;
White shirts supplied the masquerade,
And smutted cheeks the visor made
But oh! what masquers, richly dight,
Can boast of bosoms half so light!
England was merry England when
Old Christmas brought his sports again.
'twas Christmas broached the mightiest ale,
'twas Christmas told the merriest tale;
A Christmas gambol oft would cheer
A poor man's heart through half the year.

SIR WALTER SCOTT (1771–1832) BECAME POPULAR AS A POET AND
NOVELIST IN EUROPE DURING HIS LIFETIME. HE WROTE *Ivanhoe* AND
Rob Roy AND COMPILED A COLLECTION OF SCOTTISH BALLADS, *The
Minstrelsy of the Scottish Border*.

The Gift

There's a reason for the peace and joy
and love that infuse the Christmas season with
light. The baby in the manger is no ordinary baby;
he is here to change the world forever.

She will bear a son, and you are to name him Jesus,
for he will save his people from their sins.

—MATTHEW 1:21

Jesus

C. H. Spurgeon

Bernard has delightfully said that the name of Jesus is honey in the mouth, melody in the ear, and joy in the heart. . . . So inexpressibly fragrant is the name of Jesus that it imparts a delicious perfume to everything which comes in connection with it. Our thoughts will turn this morning to the first use of the name in connection with our Lord, when the child who was yet to be born was named Jesus. Here we find everything suggestive of comfort. The person to whom that name was first revealed was Joseph, a carpenter, a humble man, a working man, unknown and undistinguished save by the justice of his character. To the artizan of Nazareth was this name first imparted. It is not, therefore, a title to be monopolised by the ears of princes, sages, priests, warriors, or men of wealth: it is a name to be made a household word among common people. He is the people's Christ; for of old it was said of Him, "I have exalted one chosen out of the people." Let every carpenter, every worker of every sort, rejoice with all other sorts of men in the name of Jesus. . . .

The angel spake to him in a dream: that name is so soft and sweet that it breaks no man's rest, but rather yields a peace unrivalled, the peace of God. With such a dream Joseph's sleep was more blessed than his waking. The name has evermore this power, for, to those who know it, it unveils a glory brighter than dreams have ever imagined. Under its power young men see visions, and old men dream dreams, and these do not mock them, but are prophecies faithful and true. The name of Jesus brings before our minds a vision of glory in the latter days when Jesus shall reign from pole to pole, and yet another vision of glory unutterable when His people shall be with Him where He is. The name of Jesus was sweet at the first, because of the words with which it was accompanied; for they were meant to remove perplexity from Joseph's mind, and some of them ran thus—"Fear not." Truly, no name can banish fear like the name of Jesus: it is the beginning of hope and the end of despair. Let but the sinner hear of "the Savior," and he forgets to die, he hopes to live; he rises out of the deadly lethargy of his hopelessness, and, looking upward, he sees a reconciled God, and fears no longer. . . .

It is a name which the Holy Ghost explains, for He tells us the reason for the name of Jesus—"For He shall save His people from their sins." "Savior" is the meaning of the name, but it has a fuller sense hidden within, for in its Hebrew form it means "the salvation of the Lord," or "the Lord of salvation," or "the Savior." The angel interprets it, "he shall save," and the word for "he" is very emphatic. According to many scholars, the divine name, the incommunicable title of the Most High is contained in "Joshua," the Hebrew form of Jesus, so that in full the word means "Jehovah Savior," and in brief it signifies "Savior." It is given to our Lord because "He saves"—not according to any temporary and common salvation, from enemies and troubles, but He saves from spiritual enemies, and specially from *sins*. Joshua of old was a savior, Gideon was a savior, David was a savior; but the title is given to our Lord above all others because He is a Savior in a sense in which no one else is or can be—He saves His people from their sins. . . . Glorious beyond measure is the name "Jesus" as it is divinely expounded to us, for by that very exposition the eternal God guarantees the success of the Savior; He declares that He shall save His people, and save His people He must.✧

C.H. Spurgeon (1834–1892) was a highly popular British preacher. At one point in his career, his sermons sold more than 25,000 copies each week. He is considered one of the most widely read ministers in Christian history.

If New Testament Christianity is to reappear today with its power and joy and courage, men must recapture the basic conviction that this is a Visited planet. It is not enough to express formal belief in the "Incarnation" or in the "Divinity of Christ"; the staggering truth must be accepted afresh . . . that in this vast, mysterious universe, of which we are an almost infinitesimal part, the great Mystery, Whom we call God, has visited our planet in Person. It is from this conviction that there springs unconquerable certainty and unquenchable faith and hope.

J. B. Phillips

The Grand Miracle

C. S. Lewis

1947

The central miracle asserted by Christians is the Incarnation. They say that God became Man. Every other miracle prepares for this, or exhibits this, or results from this. Just as every natural event is the manifestation at a particular place and moment of Nature's total character, so every particular Christian miracle manifests at a particular place and moment the character and significance of the Incarnation. There is no question in Christianity of arbitrary interferences just scattered about. It relates not a series of disconnected raids on Nature but the various steps of a strategically coherent invasion—an invasion which intends complete conquest and 'occupation'. The fitness, and therefore credibility, of the particular miracles depends on their relation to the Grand Miracle; all discussion of them in isolation from it is futile.

The fitness or credibility of the Grand Miracle itself cannot, obviously, be judged by the same standard. And let us admit at once that it is very difficult to find a standard by which it can be judged. If the thing happened, it was the central event in the history of the Earth—the very thing that the whole story has been about . . . it is easier to argue, on historical grounds, that the Incarnation actually occurred than to show, on philosophical grounds, the probability of its occurrence. The historical difficulty of giving for the life, sayings and influence of Jesus any explanation that is not harder than the Christian explanation, is very great. The discrepancy between the depth and sanity and (let me add) shrewdness of His moral teaching and the rampant megalomania which must lie behind His theological teaching unless He is indeed God, has never been satisfactorily got over. ✧

C. S. Lewis (1898–1963) is possibly the most respected Christian writer of the twentieth century. He wrote more than thirty books, including *The Chronicles of Narnia* and *Mere Christianity*.

If we could condense all the truths of Christmas into only three words, these would be the words: "God with us." We tend to focus our attention at Christmas on the infancy of Christ. The greater truth of the holiday is His deity. More astonishing than a baby in the manger is the truth that this promised baby is the omnipotent Creator of the heavens and the earth!

JOHN MACARTHUR

The Angel Appears to Joseph

Now the birth of Jesus the Messiah took place in this way. When his mother Mary had been engaged to Joseph, but before they lived together, she was found to be with child from the Holy Spirit. Her husband Joseph, being a righteous man and unwilling to expose her to public disgrace, planned to dismiss her quietly. But just when he had resolved to do this, an angel of the Lord appeared to him in a dream and said, "Joseph, son of David, do not be afraid to take Mary as your wife, for the child conceived in her is from the Holy Spirit. She will bear a son, and you are to name him Jesus, for he will save his people from their sins." All this took place to fulfill what had been spoken by the Lord through the prophet:

"Look, the virgin shall conceive and bear a son, and they shall name him Emmanuel," which means, "God is with us." When Joseph awoke from sleep, he did as the angel of the Lord commanded him; he took her as his wife, but had no marital relations with her until she had borne a son; and he named him Jesus.

—Matthew 1:18–25

The Nativity

G. K. Chesterton

1927

The thatch on the roof was as golden,
Though dusty the straw was and old,
The wind had a peal as of trumpets,
Though blowing and barren and cold,
The mother's hair was a glory
Though loosened and torn,
For under the eaves in the gloaming
A child was born.

Have a myriad children been quickened,
Have a myriad children grown old,
Grown gross and unloved and embittered,
Grown cunning and savage and cold?
God abides in a terrible patience,
Unangered, unworn,
And again for the child that was squandered
A child is born.

What know we of aeons behind us,
Dim dynasties lost long ago,

Huge empires, like dreams unremembered,
Huge cities for ages laid low?
This at least—that with blight and with blessing,
With flower and with thorn,
Love was there, and his cry was among them,
"A child is born."

Though the darkness be noisy with systems,
Dark fancies that fret and disprove,
Still the plumes stir around us, above us
The wings of the shadow of love:
Oh! Princes and priests, have ye seen it
Grow pale through your scorn;
Huge dawns sleep before us, deep changes,
A child is born.

And the rafters of toil still are gilded
With the dawn of the stars of the heart,
And the wise men draw near in the twilight,
Who are weary of learning and art,
And the face of the tyrant is darkened,
His spirit is torn,
For a new king is enthroned; yea, the sternest,
A child is born.

And the mother still joys for the whispered
First stir of unspeakable things,
Still feels that high moment unfurling
Red glory of Gabriel's wings.
Still the babe of an hour is a master
Whom angels adorn,
Emmanuel, prophet, anointed,
A child is born.

And thou, that art still in thy cradle,
The sun being crown for thy brow,
Make answer, our flesh, make an answer,
Say, whence art thou come—who art thou?
Art thou come back on earth for our teaching
To train or to warn—?
Hush—how may we know?—knowing only
A child is born.✧

Take Time to Be Aware

Edward Hays

1989

Take time to be aware that in the very midst of our busy prepara-
tions for the celebration of Christ's birth in ancient Bethlehem,
Christ is reborn in the Bethlehems of our homes and daily lives. Take
time, slow down, be still, be awake to the Divine Mystery that looks
so common and so ordinary yet is wondrously present.

An old abbot was fond of saying, "The devil is always the most
active on the highest feast days."

The supreme trick of Old Scratch is to have us so busy
decorating, preparing food, practicing music and cleaning in
preparation for the feast of Christmas that we actually miss
the coming of Christ. Hurt feelings, anger, impatience, injured
egos—the list of clouds that busyness creates to blind us to the
birth can be long, but it is familiar to us all.✧

EDWARD HAYS HAS BEEN A CATHOLIC PRIEST SINCE 1958. HE HAS WRITTEN
SEVERAL BOOKS AND ESPECIALLY EMPHASIZES CONTEMPLATIVE PRAYER.

The Origin of the Christmas Crèche

Saint Bonaventure

1263

It's a part of many Christmas celebrations—the Christmas crèche, or Nativity scene, graces tables and churchyards throughout the holiday season. Saint Francis of Assisi is credited with starting the tradition, and in his The Life of Saint Francis of Assisi, *Saint Bonaventure tells us the story.*

It happened in the third year before his death, that in order to excite the inhabitants of Grecio to commemorate the nativity of the Infant Jesus with great devotion, [St. Francis] determined to keep it with all possible solemnity; and lest he should be accused of lightness or novelty, he asked and obtained the permission of the sovereign Pontiff. Then he prepared a manger, and brought hay, and an ox and an ass to the place appointed. The brethren were summoned, the people ran together, the forest resounded with their voices, and that venerable night was made glorious by many and brilliant lights and sonorous psalms of praise. The man of God [St. Francis] stood before the manger, full of devotion and piety, bathed in tears and radiant with joy; the Holy Gospel was chanted by

Francis, the Levite of Christ. Then he preached to the people around the nativity of the poor King; and being unable to utter His name for the tenderness of his love, he called Him the Babe of Bethlehem. A certain valiant and veracious soldier, Master John of Grecio, who, for the love of Christ, had left the warfare of this world, and become a dear friend of this holy man, affirmed that he beheld an Infant marvellously beautiful, sleeping in the manger, Whom the blessed Father Francis embraced with both his arms, as if he would awake Him from sleep. This vision of the devout soldier is credible, not only by reason of the sanctity of him that saw it, but by reason of the miracles which afterwards confirmed its truth. For example of Francis, if it be considered by the world, is doubtless sufficient to excite all hearts which are negligent in the faith of Christ; and the hay of that manger, being preserved by the people, miraculously cured all diseases of cattle, and many other pestilences; God thus in all things glorifying his servant, and witnessing to the great efficacy of his holy prayers by manifest prodigies and miracles.✧

SAINT BONAVENTURE (1221–1274) WAS A CATHOLIC SCHOLAR AND SAINT. HE COMPLETED THE OFFICIAL BIOGRAPHY OF THE REVERED SAINT FRANCIS—THE NAMESAKE OF THE FRANCISCAN ORDER—A FEW DECADES AFTER THE SAINT'S DEATH.

A Prayer for December 25

FROM THE BOOK OF COMMON PRAYER

Almighty God, who hast given us thy
only-begotten Son to take our nature upon him
and as at this time to be born of a pure virgin:
Grant that we, being regenerate and made thy
children by adoption and grace, may daily be
renewed by thy Holy Spirit; through the same
our Lord Jesus Christ, who liveth and reigneth
with thee and the same Spirit ever, one God,
world without end. Amen.

A Christmas Carol for Children

Martin Luther

1534

Good news from heaven the angels bring,
Glad tidings to the earth they sing:
To us this day a child is given,
To crown us with the joy of heaven.

This is the Christ, our God and Lord,
Who in all need shall aid afford:
He will Himself our Saviour be,
From sin and sorrow set us free.

To us that blessedness He brings,
Which from the Father's bounty springs:
That in the heavenly realm we may
With Him enjoy eternal day.

All hail, Thou noble Guest, this morn,
Whose love did not the sinner scorn!
In my distress Thou cam'st to me:
What thanks shall I return to Thee?

Were earth a thousand times as fair,
Beset with gold and jewels rare,
She yet were far too poor to be
A narrow cradle, Lord, for Thee.

Ah, dearest Jesus, Holy Child!
Make Thee a bed, soft, undefiled,
Within my heart, that it may be
A quiet chamber kept for Thee.

Praise God upon His heavenly throne,
Who gave to us His only Son:
For this His hosts, on joyful wing,
A blest New Year of mercy sing.

MARTIN LUTHER (1483–1546) WAS A GERMAN MONK AND THEOLOGIAN
TO WHOM THE START OF THE PROTESTANT REFORMATION IS LARGELY
CREDITED. HE WROTE SEVERAL WORKS, INCLUDING HYMNS AND A
TRANSLATION OF THE NEW TESTAMENT INTO COMMON GERMAN.

Special Ways to Use *A Classic Christmas*

As an Advent Devotional

Many Christians plan daily devotions for the twenty-five days that end on Christmas morning. The range of spiritual and reflective materials found in *A Classic Christmas* are ideal for this purpose. Below is a suggested reading plan, but you can mix and match passages or add others as you see fit.

December 1: The Angel Appears to Mary, Luke 1:26–38

December 2: In the Bleak Midwinter by Christina Rossetti

December 3: Our Christmas Meditation by E. Stanley Jones

December 4: A Christmas Inspiration by Lucy Maud Montgomery

December 5: Never Alone by Henri Nouwen

December 6: Christmas Everywhere by Phillips Brooks

December 7: The Angel Appears to Joseph, Matthew 1:18–25

December 8: The Nativity by G. K. Chesterton

December 9: The Origin of the Christmas Crèche by Saint Bonaventure

December 10: The Journey of the Maji, Matthew 2:1-12

December 11: The Nativity by Rudyard Kipling

December 12: The First Christmas Tree by Eugene Field

December 13: The Servant of the Lord, Isaiah 61:1-3

December 14: Mary's Song of Praise, Luke 1:46-55

December 15: Swaddling Clothes by Karl Barth

December 16: The Grand Miracle by C. S. Lewis

December 17: The Other Wise Man by Henry Van Dyke

December 18: Sermon on Advent Sunday (December 2, 1928) by Dietrich Bonhoeffer

December 19: A Christmas Carol for Children by Martin Luther

December 20: Christmas by Frederick Buechner

December 21: Jesus by C. H. Spurgeon

December 22: Mary by Thomas Merton

December 23: The Angel Song of Praise by Martin Luther

December 24: God Comes by Pope Benedict XVI

December 25: The Birth of Jesus, Luke 2:1–21

As a Family Reader

Reading together is a powerful way to knit your family together in spirit and love during the Christmas season. You can follow the Advent schedule above or put more emphasis on literature and legends. A parent might lead this family gathering, but it would be good to consider having a child select one evening's reading selection and have the honor of reading aloud to family.

Church and Small Groups

The material in *A Classic Christmas* is wonderful for illustration or as a thematic basis for a worship service or small group discussion time. There are also some creative ways to include others in presenting the material. For example, selections like "A Christmas Inspiration" by Lucy Maud Montgomery, "The Other Wise Man" by Henry Van Dyke, and "Christmas Day in the Morning" by Pearl S. Buck would be great as a "theater in the round," where the passage is read dramatically with different individuals assigned to characters.

Parties and Celebrations

Why do we get together as work colleagues, neighborhoods, friends, and families? To connect, of course. You might have a short, favorite selection from *A Classic Christmas*. Consider reading it aloud during a moment when you pull everyone together from mingling to welcome and acknowledge your guests.

Share with Others

Consider making a Christmas visit to a nursing home or the home of an elderly neighbor or fellow parishioner to spend time with someone who is lonely during this season. That person might like having you read aloud to him or her.

Index of Authors

Index of Works

Acknowledgments
and Permissions

"Advent Meditations" from *A Year with Pope John Paul II* (New York: HarperOne, 2005). Copyright © 2005 the K. S. Giniger Company. Used by permission. All rights reserved.

"Christmas" from *Beyond Words* by Frederick Buechner (New York: HarperOne, 2004). Copyright © 2004 by Frederick Buechner. Used by permission. All rights reserved.

"Christmas 1943" from *The Journey Back from Hell: An Oral History with Concentration Camp Survivors* by Anton Gill (New York: Morrow, 1988). Copyright © 1988 by Anton Gill. Used by permission. All rights reserved.

"Christmas and the Professors" by G. K. Chesterton. *Illustrated London News* 18 December 1909. Copyright © 1909 by G.K. Chesterton. All rights reserved.

"Christmas Bells" from *The Home Book of Verse*, vol. 1 (New York: Henry Holt and Company, 1912). Copyright © 1864 by Henry Wadsworth Longfellow. All rights reserved.